NINETY NINE NAMES
OF
ALLĀH

TRANSLITERATION
ENGLISH TRANSLATION WITH
EXPLANATORY NOTES

MUHAMMAD IQBAL SIDDIQI

KAZI PUBLICATIONS

2

Composed & Designed by:

ASIM Composing & Printing Associates,
114-Zulqarnain Chambers, Ganpat Road,
Anarkali, Lahore — Pakistan PH: 322656

PUBLISHED BY

KAZI Publications, 121-Zulqarnain Chambers
Ganpat Road, Lahore (Pakistan) Ph : 61893

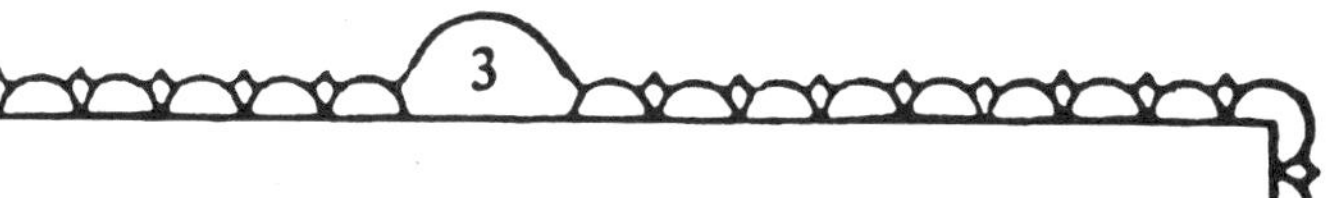

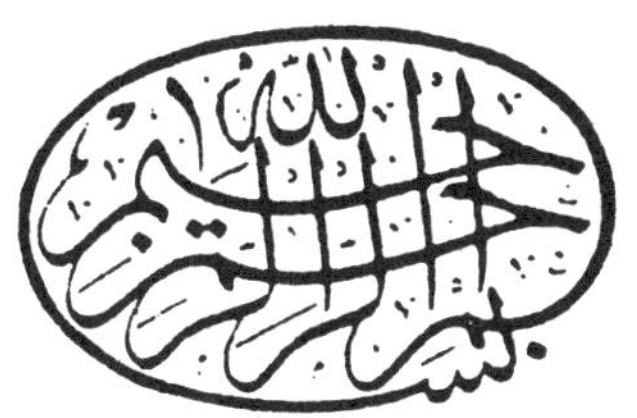

ALLAH'S ARE THE EXCELLENT NAMES
INVOKE HIM BY THEM (7 : 180)

عَنْ اَبِىْ هُرَيْرَةَ عَنِ النَّبِيِّ صَلَّىَ اللّـهُ عَلَيْهِ وَسَـلَّمَ قَالَ اِنَّ لِلّٰهِ تِسْعَـةً وَتِسْعِيْنَ اِسْمًا مَّنْ حَفِظَهَا دَخَلَ الْجَنَّةَ ـ (مسلم)

Abu Hurairah (Allāh be pleased with him) reported Allāh's Messenger (peace and blessings of Allāh be upon him) as saylng: There are ninety nine names of Allāh; he who commits them to memory would get into paradise (*Muslim*)

CONTENTS

FOREWORD

The Holy Qur'ān enjoins on us to recite the Names of Allāh in the following verses :

$$\text{وَلِلّٰهِ الْاَسْمَآءُ الْحُسْنٰى فَادْعُوْهُ بِهَاص}$$

Allāh's are the Excellent Names, therefore invoke Him therewith. (7 : 180)

$$\text{قُلِ ادْعُوا اللّٰهَ اَوِ ادْعُوا الرَّحْمٰنَ اَيًّا مَّا تَدْعُوْا فَلَهُ الْاَسْمَآءُ الْحُسْنٰى}$$

Say : Call upon Allāh, or call upon Rahmān: by whatever name ye call upon Him, (it is well): for to Him belong the Most Beautiful Names. (17 : 110)

$$\text{هُوَ اللّٰهُ الْخَالِقُ الْبَارِئُ الْمُصَوِّرُ لَهُ الْاَسْمَآءُ الْحُسْنٰى يُسَبِّحُ لَهُ مَا فِى السَّمٰوٰتِ وَالْاَرْضِ وَهُوَ الْعَزِيْزُ الْحَكِيْمُ}$$

He is Allāh, the Creator, the Evolver, the Bestower of Forms (or Colours). To Him b: ·

long the Most Beautiful Names, whatever is in the heavens and on earth, doth declare His Praises and Glory: and He is the Exalted in Might, the Wise. (59 : 24)

اللهُ لَآ اِلٰهَ اِلَّا هُوَ لَهُ الْاَسْمَآءُ الْحُسْنٰى

Allāh! there is no god but He. To Him belong the Most Beautiful Names. (20 : 8)

We all praise Allāh and solicit His blessings for His kind Messenger Muhammad for the True knowledge of Allāh and His attributes have come to us through him. He taught us that Allāh is the only One God, Who has ninety-nine attributive names. "Allāh" is a proper noun par excellence in a consolidated form meaning "God". No plural can be formed out of it nor any derivation is possible. It connotes the attributes of Perfection and Beauty. Allāh is the name of the Divine One, as distinguished from all other attributive names called *Asmā-ul-Husna*, the most excellent names. There are ninety-nine Epithets of His attributes mentioned through the Holy Qur'ān.

One Name which has been hidden by Allāh is called *Ismu'l A'zam:* The Sublimest Name of Allāh. There is difference of opinion regarding the Greatest Name of Allāh among the jurists.

It has also been said that *Ismu'l A'zam* is that Name of Allāh which appears to an individual most appealing to move towards God. The latter seems to be in consonance with reason.

hidden this particular Name it is referred to as the Sublimest Name. According to the following Traditions, the Almighty has an "Exalted Name" known as the *Ismu'l A'zam*, which the Messenger of Allāh (peace and blessings of Allāh be upon him) is reported to have said was either in the *Surah al-Baqarah* or in the *Surah Al-i-'Imran*:

Asmā' bint Yazid (Allāh be pleased with her) reported that the Messenger of Allāh (peace and blessings of Allāh be upon him) said : The Greatest Name of Allāh is in these two verses (of the Holy Qur'ān) :

$$وَإِلٰهُكُمْ اِلٰهٌ وَّاحِدٌ ۚ لَّا اِلٰهَ اِلَّا هُوَ الرَّحْمٰنُ الرَّحِيْمُ$$

And your God is One God. There is no god save Him, the Beneficent, the Merciful. (2 : 163)

and also in the first part of *Surah Al-i-'Imran:*

$$الٓمّٓ ۚ اللّٰهُ لَا اِلٰهَ اِلَّا هُوَ الْحَيُّ الْقَيُّوْمُ*$$

ALIF. LĀM. MIM. God! save Him there is no other god, the Living, the Eternal. (3 : 1)

(Tirmidhi, Abū Dāwūd, Ibn Majah and Darimi)

The Names of Allāh which occur in these two verses of the Holy Qur'ān are *ar-Rahmān*, "The Merciful", *ar-Rahim*, "The Compassionate," *al-Haiy*, "The Living", and *al-Qaiyūm* "The Subsisting."

Anas (Allāh be pleased with him) reported: Whilst

I was sitting with the Messenger of Allāh (peace and blessings of Allāh be upon him) in the mosque, a man was offering *Salāt* (Prayer). (In the course of his prayer) the man said :

$$\text{اَللّٰهُمَّ اِنِّيْ اَسْئَلُكَ بِاَنَّ لَكَ الْحَمْدُ لَآ اِلٰهَ اَنْتَ الْحَنَّانُ الْمَنَّانُ بَدِيْعُ السَّمٰوٰتِ وَالْاَرْضِ يَا ذَا الْجَلَالِ وَ الْاِكْرَامِ يَا حَيُّ يَا قَيُّوْمُ اَسْئَلُكَ}$$

O' God! Behold, I beg of Thee because unto Thee belongeth all praise. There is no god save Thee, the Most Relenting, the Most Bountiful, the Originator of the heavens and the earth. O' Lord of Majesty and Glory, O' Living, Eternal One, of Thee I beg !

whereupon the Messenger of Allāh (peace and blessings of Allāh be upon him) said : (This man) invoked Allāh by His sublimest name. When He is called upon by that name He respondeth, and when He is besought in that name He bestoweth. *(Tirmidhi, Abū Dāwūd, Nasa'i and Ibn Majah)*

There is, however, another tradition, from which it would appear that the name may be either *al-Ahad*, "The One", or *as-Samad*, "The Eternal".

Buraida (Allāh be pleased with him) reported that the Messenger of Allāh (peace and blessings of Allāh be upon him) heard a man saying :

اَللّٰهُمَّ اِنِّىْ اَسْئَلُكَ بِاَنَّكَ اَنْتَ اللهُ لَاۤ

اِلٰهَ اَنْتَ الْاَحَدُ الصَّمَدُ الَّذِىْ لَمْ

يَلِدْ وَلَمْ يُوْلَدْ وَلَمْ يَكُنْ لَهُ كُفُوًا

اَحَدٌ

O' God! Behold, I beg of Thee, because Thou art God. There is no god save Thee, the One, the Eternal Support of the Creation, Who neither begettest nor wast Begotten. There is none like unto Him.

whereupon he said : (This man) has beseeched Allāh by His sublimest name. When He is besought in that name, He bestoweth, and when He is invoked by that name, He respondeth. *(Tirmidhi* and *Abū Dāwūd)*

Abdul Haq in his remarks on these traditions, says that it is generally held, according to a tradition by 'Ā'isha (Allāh be pleased with her), that this great name is known only to the prophets and other saintly persons. The Compiler of the *Kitābu't Ta'rifāt* says it is none other than the name of Allāh.

'Ā'isha (Allāh be pleased with her) mentioned that *Ya Rabb* (O' Lord) is the Greatest Name of Allāh.

The order adopted by the Holy Qur'ān in speaking of the Divine Attributes is a highly scientific one. Allāh (the *Ismu'l-A'zam)* comes first in the opening Chapter of Qur'ān, and is followed by *Rabb*, the most important of the attributive names. *Rabb*, the Sustainer, and not

Abb or Father, which has its own limitations. Allāh has no consort nor has He a son (6 : 10). Next in importance to *Rabb*, are the names *Rahmān, Rahim* and *Mālik* which follow *Rabb* in the opening Chapter. These three names, in fact, show how the attribute of *Ra-boo-bi-yah*, or bringing to perfection by fostering, is brought into play.

The essential difference between a judge and a master is that the former is found to do justice and must punish the evil-doer while the latter, the master, can exercise his discretion, and may either punish the evil-doer or forgive him, as in the verse below:

$$\text{قُلْ يٰعِبَادِىَ الَّذِينَ اَسْرَفُوْا عَلٰى اَنْفُسِهِمْ لَا تَقْنَطُوْا مِنْ رَّحْمَةِ اللّٰهِ اِنَّ اللّٰهَ يَغْفِرُ الذُّنُوْبَ جَمِيْعًا اِنَّهٗ هُوَ الْغَفُوْرُ الرَّحِيْمُ}$$

Say : O' my Servants who have transgressed against their souls ! despair not of the Mercy of Allāh : for Allāh forgives all sins, for He is Oft-Forgiving, Most Merciful. (39 : 53)

All the attributes of Allāh are absolute. The attribute of His perfection possesses a distinct glory and reveals Him as the Light wherein there is no darkness at all. Like the prismatic colours each distinct, and in the utmost perfection of beauty yet all blending in one beam of life and light.

Power is the glorious attribute of Allāh Almighty

which furnishes the rest of His perfections. It is His Omnipotence that makes His wisdom and goodness effectual to the measure of His Will. Thus His decrees are immutable and His Commands unalterable. It is this which has brought forth all creation at His first call : He uttered the word *kun* and they came to life and in position.

There is all possible perfection in God. In Him is absolute fulness. The source of All Life is God. All wisdom is in God. He is the Wise. All purity is in God. All righteousness is in God.

His ninety-nine attributes are not only individually complete but perfect in their harmony. They combine as the prismatic colours in light and unite as the several elements which constitute the atmosphere and blend as the hues of the rainbow.

He is the Affectionate, Loving, Kind, Benign, Oft-Returning to mercy, and Multiplier of rewards, Author of peace, Granter of security. Though He made great things like the sun and the stars, yet He thinks much more of us men, than He does of others. He made the others for our benefit. Not even the smallest flower or the tiniest bird is ever out of God's sight. He is the Creator. He is the Almighty.

His name is Allāh, and we can call on Him by other sacred names also which are attributive or qualitative with great benefits and blessings. Nevertheless, He must be remembered, or called upon only with one of the names by which the last Prophet and Guide, Muhammad (peace and blessings of Allāh be upon him) is known to have remembered or called on Him. The reason for this is simple. Allah Almighty is beyond human comprehension and, therefore, to call on Him by names out of one's own imagination may be unbecoming to His Omnipotence.

It has come down to us from the Holy Prophet (peace and blessings of Allāh be upon him) that Allāh Almighty has ninety-nine auspicious Names :

Abu Huraira (Allāh be pleased with him) reported Allāh's Messenger (peace and blessings of Allāh be upon him) as saying : There are ninety-nine names of Allāh ; he who commits them to memory would get into Paradise. Verily, Allāh is Odd (He is One and it is an odd number) and He loves odd number. And in the narration of Ibn 'Umar (Allāh be pleased with him) the words are : "He who enumerated them." *(Muslim)*

Abu Huraira (Allāh be pleased with him) reported Allāh's Messenger (peace and blessings of Allāh be upon him) as saying: Verily, there are ninety-nine names for Allāh, *i.e.,* hundred excepting one. He who enumerates them would get into Paradise. And Hammam has made this addition on the authority of Abu Huraira (Allāh be pleased with him) who reported it from Allāh's Messenger (peace and blessings of Allāh be upon him) that he said : "He is Odd (One) and loves odd number." *(Muslim)*

Islam has greatly stressed on its followers the need of remembering Allāh, as it is the soul of the true life of man both in this world and in the Hereafter.

The Qur'ān and Ahādith are full of instructions which insist on the faithful to see that their heart is always adored with the remembrance of Allāh.

Man's heart is full of foul and frivolous thoughts, temptations, vices etc., and the remembrance of Allāh is the cure for the diseased condition of our hearts. The more we remember Allāh the better will be the condition of our hearts, and above all by continuous remembrance we will be able to create the fear of Allāh, which serves as a guiding force in our march on the path of Truth. Remembrance of Allāh is an act which brings Divine blessings and also great reward. Allāh says :

$$فَاذْكُرُوْنِيْ أَذْكُرْكُمْ وَاشْكُرُوْا لِيْ وَلَا تَكْفُرُوْنِ ٥$$

Therefore, remember Me and I will remember you; and be thankful unto Me and be you not ungrateful towards Me. (2 : 152)
Again He says :

$$وَاذْكُرْ رَّبَّكَ فِيْ نَفْسِكَ تَضَرُّعًا وَّخِيْفَةً وَّدُوْنَ الْجَهْرِ مِنَ الْقَوْلِ بِالْغُدُوِّ وَالْاٰصَالِ وَلَا تَكُنْ مِّنَ الْغٰفِلِيْنَ ٥ اِنَّ الَّذِيْنَ عِنْدَ رَبِّكَ لَا يَسْتَكْبِرُوْنَ$$

And do thou (O' reader!) bring thy Lord to remembrance in thy (very) soul with humility and in reverence, without loudness in words, in the mornings and evenings; and be not thou of those who are unheedful. (7 : 205)

Other verses on remembrance of Allāh are also quoted below : —

الَّذِيْنَ اٰمَنُوْا وَتَطْمَئِنُّ قُلُوْبُهُمْ بِذِكْرِ اللهِ ۗ اَلَا بِذِكْرِ اللهِ تَطْمَئِنُّ الْقُلُوْبُ ۝

Those who believe, and whose hearts find satisfaction in the remembrance of Allāh: for without doubt in the remembrance of Allāh do hearts find satisfaction. (13 : 28)

وَلَذِكْرُ اللهِ اَكْبَرُ ۗ

And remembrance of Allāh is the greatest (thing in life) without doubt. (29 : 45)

يَاۤ اَيُّهَا الَّذِيْنَ اٰمَنُوا اذْكُرُوا اللهَ ذِكْرًا كَثِيْرًا ۝

O' You who believe ! Celebrate the praises of Allāh, and do this often. (33 : 41)

The above Verses clearly ordain the faithful to remember Allāh. Among the benefits that accrue from this deed is contentment, blessings, piety, strengthening of faith and abstention from evils and vices. And the best of all is that Allāh remembers us, a kindness which can altogether change the trend of life to the best advantage of the believers both here and in the Hereafter.

The Holy Prophet (peace and blessings of Allāh be upon him) again and again instructed and advised his companions to keep their hearts always illuminated with the remembrance of Allāh. According to him, the heart is the source of good and bad thoughts and deeds and when there is slackness on the part of a believer in the remembrance of Allāh, bad ideas and thoughts occur in it and ultimately they result in sins or vices. When the remembrance of Allāh is in abundance, bad thoughts and ideas are suppressed and good ones occur which lead to good deeds.

Ibn 'Abbas (Allāh be pleased with him) reported the Messenger of Allāh (peace and blessings of Allāh be upon him) as saying : Satan is holding fast man's heart and when man remembers Allāh, he leaves (the heart) and when man becomes careless in remembrance he begins to create ill feelings. *(Bukhāri).*

The Messenger of Allāh (peace and blessings of Allāh be upon him) also said that everything has a polish and the polish of heart is the remembrance of Allāh. *(Baihaqi)*

In short, the remembrance of Allāh is the happiest and also the wisest of pastime. Its blessings can never be counted and the satisfaction it brings cannot be measured. We should always keep ourselves busy in the remembrance of Allāh, even while doing our work, business and other works. The act of remembrance will save us from bad thoughts and vices and improve both our spiritual and worldly life. Briefly it relieves one of the worries that otherwise eat into one's heart. We wish that our readers will make it a point to recite the Holy Names of Allāh regularly together with the recitation of the Holy Qur'an, morning and evening for peace and heartfelt satisfaction.

In this book brief explanatory notes on *Asmā-ul-Husna* are given. If some readers are pleased with my humble effort, I entreat them to remember me in their prayers for my spiritual advancement and atonement. I also admit that I might have made some unintentional mistakes for which, in all humility, I seek pardon and forgiveness.

In the end I must express my thanks to my younger brother Prof. Muhammad Ikram Siddiqi who went through the manuscript and gave some valuable suggestions for its improvement and to my nephew Mr. Nisar Ahmad Siddiqi and Mr. Ghulam Ali who typed the manuscript with a commendable spirit of devotion. I am also indebted to Ch. Mohammad Hussain who took considerable pains in doing the tedious job of proof-reading. May Allāh, the Almighty, reward all of them for their kind help and assistance.

MUHAMMAD IQBAL SIDDIQI

LAHORE
31st January, 1987.

ALLAH

GOD

اِنَّنِىٓ اَنَا اللّٰهُ لَآ اِلٰهَ اِلَّآ اَنَا فَاعۡبُدۡنِىۡ وَاَقِمِ الصَّلٰوةَ لِذِكۡرِىۡ ٥

Lo! I, even I, am Allāh. There is no god save Me. So serve Me and establish worship for My remembrance. (20 : 14)

The term Allāh is the proper name for the Creator and Sustainer Whose Will reigns supreme in the universe and Who alone is worthy of the highest honour, the greatest respect and admiration and is the sole object of worship. The word is in fact incapable of translation and the other words like God, Deity are poor substitutes for it. It is not a common noun meaning a god or a divine being. It is a proper noun *par excellence*. No plural can be derived from it and it has, according to the best authorities, no root and derivation. The word connotes all attributes of perfection and beauty in their infinitude and denotes none but the One and Unique God, the Supreme, Perfect, Tender, Mighty, Most Gracious, Most Benign and Compassionate.

The title *Allāh* is called the *Ism az-Zat*, or the essential name of God, all other titles including *Rabb*, being considered *Asmā' as-Sifat*, or "attributes" of the Divine Being. Then attributes are called *al-Asmā' al-Husna* or the "Excellent Names". This expression occurs in the Holy Qur'an as follows:

$$\text{وَلِلّٰهِ الْأَسْمَاءُ الْحُسْنَى فَادْعُوهُ بِهَا ص}$$

Allah's are the Excellent Names. Invoke Him by them. (7 : 180)

This verse is commented upon in the Tradition:

Abu Hurairah (Allāh be pleased with him) reported Allāh's Messenger (peace and blessings of Allāh be upon him) as saying: There are ninety-nine names of Allāh; he who commits them to memory would get into paradise. *(Muslim)*

ASMĀ'-ULLAH-I-TA'ALA

THE ATTRIBUTES OF ALLĀH THE EXALTED

AR-RAHMAN

THE COMPASSIONATE

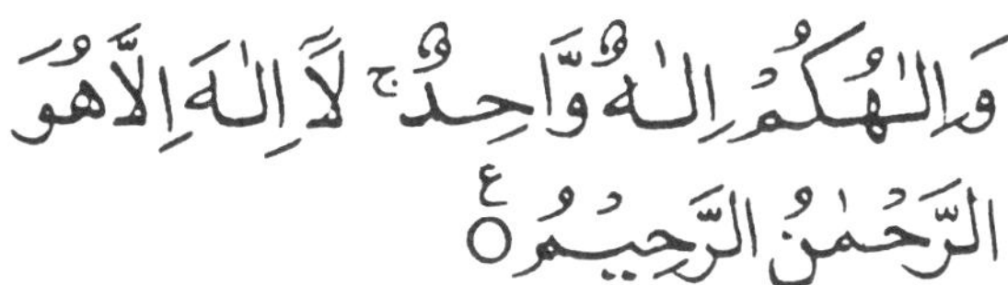

Your God is One God; there is no gad save
Him, the Compassionate, the Merciful. (2 : 163)

The term *Rahman* is derived from *Rahmat*. The term *Rahmat* in Arabic is used to denote the type of tenderness which stimulates in one the urge to show kindness to others. Its connotation is wide enough to cover the qualities of love, compassion, benevolence and generosity. *Ar-Rahman* means the Being overflowing with the quality of mercy and always ready to pour it out upon His creation. Allāh is *Ar-Rahman* because He gives blessings and prosperity to all beings without any disparity.

Al-Baidawi says that *Ar-Rahman* is a more exalted attribute than *ar-Rahim*, because it not only contains five letters whilst *Rahim* only has four, but it expresses that universal attribute of mercy which the Almighty Allāh extends to all mankind, the wicked and the good, believers and unbelievers.

He who repeats this Name 100 times after each *Fard* (Obligatory) Prayer will have good memory, a keen awareness, and be free of a heavy heart.

AR-RAHIM
THE MERCIFUL

Praise be to Allāh, Lord of the Worlds: The Compassionate, the Merciful. (1 : 1, 2)

The Arabic words *Rahman* and *Rahim*, translated "Most Compassionate" and "Most Merciful" are both intensive forms of referring to different aspects of God's attribute of Mercy. The Arabic intensive is more suited to express God's attributes than the superlative degree in English. The latter implies a comparison with other beings, or with other times or places, while there is no being like unto God, and He is independent of Time and Place. Mercy may imply pity, long-suffering patience, and forgiveness, all of which the sinner needs and God Most Merciful bestows in abundant measure. But there is Mercy that goes before even the need arises, the Grace which is ever watchful and flows from God Most Gracious to all His creatures, protecting them, preserving them, guiding them, and leading them to clearer light and higher life. For this reason the attribute *Rahman* (Most Compassionate) is not applied to any but God and the attribute *Rahim* (Most Merciful) is a general term, and may also be applied to men.

God's mercy is in and for all things. All nature subserves a common purpose, which is for the good of all His creatures. Our faculties and our understanding are all instances of His grace and mercy. Each unit or factor among His creatures benefits from the others and receives them as God's mercy to itself; and in its turn, each contributes to the benefit of the others and is thus an instance of God's mercy to them. His mercy is universal and all-pervasive, while His justice and punishment are reserved for those who swerve from His plan and go out of His Peace.

He who repeats this Name 100 times after each *Fajr* (Morning) Prayer will find everyone to be friendly towards him.

AL-MĀLIK
THE SOVEREIGN

فَتَعَالَى اللهُ الْمَلِكُ الْحَقُّ ۚ

Then exalted be Allāh, the True Sovereign.
(20 : 114)

Al-Mālik is a name of the All-Powerful Being, Who is Sovereign, King and Ruler of all the Creations. Literally the word *Mālik* means King. It is one of the Attributes of Allāh which means the King of all the kings. Allāh is the Sole Sovereign of the whole human race. He is the Maker and Master of all created things. He is the True Ruler of this world and the world Hereafter. Allāh, the Almighty sways not only over this entire world but also over all the other worlds and creations. He is the One and the only real King, Who will remain for ever, and Who rules not merely over the bodies of all beings but even over their hearts and spirits. Hence He is called *Al-Mālik*.

He who repeats this Name will be respected by others.

AL-QUDDŪS

THE HOLY

الْقُدُّوسُ جَلَّ جَلَالُهُ

هُوَاللهُ الَّذِى لَآ اِلٰهَ اِلَّاهُوَ اَلْمَلِكُ
الْقُدُّوسُ

He is Allāh, than Whom there is no other god,
the Sovereign Lord, the Holy One. (59 : 23)

Al-Quddūs is another Attribute of Allāh which conveys the meaning and sense of purity in all respects that is to say : Allāh is Pure and free from all sorts of drawbacks, faults, flaws, defects, blemishes etc., that are found in human beings because He is like no other being and no other being is like Him. He is the Perfect Holy Supreme Being Who will remain for ever. Jibra'il and other angels are called *Quddūsi* as they are considered pure, innocent and free from human drawbacks and flaws, but their purity is in no way comparable with the purity and other attributes of the Omnipotent Being which are above everything and cannot be encompassed by worldly understanding and wisdom. Allāh is *Al-Quddūs* because He is above all human weaknesses.

The hearts of those who repeat this Name 100 times daily will be free from anxiety.

AS-SALĀM

THE AUTHOR OF SAFETY

هُوَ ٱللّٰهُ ٱلَّذِى لَاۤ إِلَٰهَ إِلَّا هُوَ ٱلْمَلِكُ الْقُدُّوسُ السَّلَٰمُ

He is Allāh, than Whom there is no other god,
the Sovereign Lord, the Holy One, the Author
of Safety. (59 : 23)

Salām is the proper name for Allāh. It means security in its entirety, free from any hazard and decline. The name *Salām* manifests that all His obedient servants are protected and endowed with security by Him. When the angel Jibra'il conveyed greetings from Allāh and from himself to Hadrat Khadija (Allāh be pleased with her) wife of the Messenger of Allāh (peace and blessings of Allāh be upon him), she said in reply that they get security from Almighty Allāh alone. It is also obligatory

on all the individuals of Muslim *Ummah* that on hearing or uttering the name of the Holy Prophet Muhammad they must send *Salāt* and *Salām* (peace and blessings of Allāh) upon him. It means peace *i.e.*, Who is perfect in peace. One Who confers peace upon others. It was the wont of the Holy Prophet (peace and blessings of Allāh be upon him) to supplicate the following *Du'a* at the end of every obligatory Prayer (*Salāt*):

$$ \text{اَللّٰهُمَّ اَنْتَ السَّلَامُ وَمِنْكَ السَّلَامُ} $$
$$ \text{تَبَارَكْتَ يَا ذَا الْجَلَالِ وَالْاِكْرَامِ} $$

O' Allāh! Thou art the Peace and from Thee is the peace. Blessed art Thou, O' Lord of Majesty and Glory.

Din with Allāh is *al-Islām.* Islām is the name of the Religion selected and favoured by Allāh, its meaning being to bow down before Him. It is closely related with His name *Salām.*

He who repeats this Name 160 times to a sick person will help him regain health.

AL-MU'MIN

THE GIVER OF PEACE جَلَّ جَلَالُهُ اَلْمُؤْمِن

هُوَاللهُ الَّذِىْ لَا اِلٰهَ اِلَّا هُوَ اَلْمَلِكُ الْقُدُّوُسُ السَّلٰمُ الْمُؤْمِن

He is Allāh, than Whom there is no other god, the Sovereign Lord, the Holy One, the Author of Safety, the Giver of Peace. (59 : 23)

One of the Attributes of Allāh is *Mu'min*. It has two meanings.

(a) Allāh is *Mu'min* because He bestows *'Imam* (Faith).

وَلٰكِنَّ اللهَ حَبَّبَ اِلَيْكُمُ الْاِيْمَانَ

But Allāh has endeared the faith to you. (49 : 7)
Again the Holy Qur'ān says :

أُولٰٓئِكَ كَتَبَ فِىْ قُلُوْبِهِمُ الْاِيْمَانَ

For such He has written faith in their hearts.

(58 : 22)

(b) Secondly Allāh is *Mu'min* because He is the Giver of Peace. The Holy Qur'ān says:

وَكَيْفَ اَخَافُ مَاۤ اَشْرَكْتُمْ وَلَا
تَخَافُوْنَ اَنَّكُمْ اَشْرَكْتُمْ بِاللّٰهِ مَا
لَمْ يُنَزِّلْ بِهٖ عَلَيْكُمْ سُلْطٰنًا ۚ فَاَىُّ
الْفَرِيْقَيْنِ اَحَقُّ بِالْاَمْنِ ۚ اِنْ كُنْتُمْ
تَعْلَمُوْنَ ۟ اَلَّذِيْنَ اٰمَنُوْا وَلَمْ يَلْبِسُوْا
اِيْمَانَهُمْ بِظُلْمٍ اُولٰٓئِكَ لَهُمُ الْاَمْنُ
وَهُمْ مُّهْتَدُوْنَ ۟

*How should I fear (the things) ye associ-
ate with Allāh, when ye fear not to give
partners to Allāh without any warrant
having been given to you? Which of (us)
two parties hath more right to security?
(Tell me) if ye know. It is those who believe and confuse not their beliefs with
wrong that are (truly) to security, for
they are on (right) guidance. (6 : 81, 82)*

Thus Allāh is *Mu'min* because He is the Bestower of Faith and the Giver of Peace.

He who recites this Name will be secure from harm.

AL-MUHAIMIN
THE PROTECTOR 

هُوَ اللهُ الَّذِى لَا اِلٰهَ اِلَّا هُوَ اَلْمَلِكُ الْقُدُّوسُ السَّلٰمُ الْمُؤْمِنُ الْمُهَيْمِنُ

He is Allāh, than Whom there is no other god, the Sovereign Lord, the Holy One, the Author of Safety, the Giver of Peace, the Protector.
(59 : 23)

Al-Muhaimin is another Attribute of Allāh which means the Protector or the Guardian just like a bird safeguarding and protecting its young ones under cover of its feathers. Protection, safeguarding, and preservation are such qualities which are greatly manifested by the name *Muhamin* of the Omnipotent Being. Allāh is *Muhaimin* because He protects us from all sorts of dangers. He grants us our rights and dispels of fears and hazards. Therefore, *Muhaimin* is the name of Allāh containing all these attributes.

Muhaimin is also used for the Holy Qur'ān in the following verse :

وَاَنْزَلْنَا اِلَيْكَ الْكِتٰبَ بِالْحَقِّ مُصَدِّقًا لِّمَا بَيْنَ يَدَيْهِ مِنَ الْكِتٰبِ وَمُهَيْمِنًا

عَلَيْهِ

To thee We sent the Scripture in truth,
confirming the scripture that came
before it, and guarding it in safety.(5 : 48)

Here it means that after the corruption of the older revelations, the Holy Qur'ān comes with a two-fold purpose : (1) to confirm the true and original Message, and (2) to guard it, or act as check to its interpretations. Thus the Holy Qur'ān has safeguarded and preserved the revelations contained in the preceding Divine Book *viz.*, *Zabur*, *Torah* and *Injil*.

Those who recite this Name with full attentiveness, their inner being will be luminous.

AL-'AZIZ

THE MIGHTY ONE

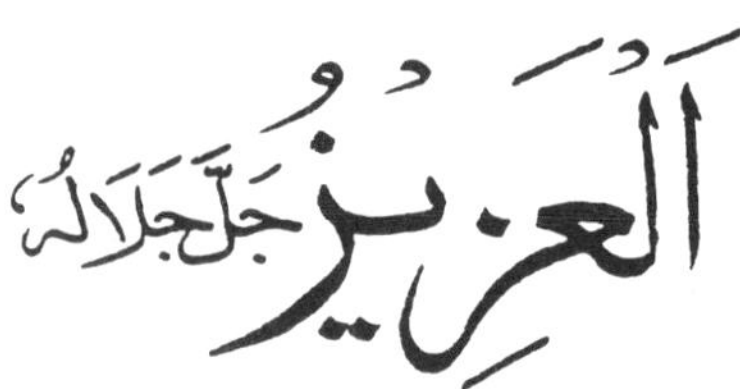

He is Allāh, than Whom there is no other god, the Sovereign Lord, the Holy One, the Author of Safety, the Giver of Peace, the Protector, the Mighty One. (59 : 23)

Al-'Aziz means Exalted in power, rank, dignity; Incomparable; Full of might and majesty; Able to enforce His will. It is derived from the word *'Izat* which means dignity, majesty and power. Thus *'Aziz* is One Who has all such attributes. The infidels named a deity as *'Azza.* This is feminine form of the word *'Aziz.* Allāh is called *Al-'Aziz* because He is Strong and Sovereign. He is holding command over the Heavens and Earth and whatso is between them. His Hand is over all His Works.

He who repeats this Name 40 times after *Fajr* (Morning) Prayer for 40 days will not only become self-sufficient but will be independent of need from others.

AL-JABBĀR
THE COMPELLER

*He is Allāh, than Whom there is no other god,
the Sovereign Lord, the Holy One, the Author
of Safety, the Giver of Peace, the Protector,
the Mighty One, the Compeller. (59 : 23)*

It is derived from *Jabbār* which means correctitude. When this word is used in the case of a human being it means one who is arrogant, haughty, hard-hearted and cruel. But as an Attribute of Allāh it means the Comforter of dishearted persons.

He who recites this Name will not be compelled to do anything against his wishes, and will not be exposed to violence, severity, or hardness.

AL-MUTAKABBIR

THE MAJESTIC

هُوَاللهُ الَّذِىْ لَآ اِلٰهَ اِلَّا هُوَ اَلْمَلِكُ الْقُدُّوسُ السَّلٰمُ الْمُؤْمِنُ الْمُهَيْمِنُ الْعَزِيْزُ الْجَبَّارُ الْمُتَكَبِّرُ ط

*He is Allāh, than Whom there is no other god,
the Sovereign Lord, the Holy One, the Author
of Safety, the Giver of Peace, the Protector,
the Mighty One, the Compeller, the Majestic.
(59 : 23)*

This word is derived from *Kibbar* which means
majesty. It is Allāh Who is the true Majestic. He is above
all. He shows His greatness in all things and in all ways.
None is "great" except the Greatest One.

He who repeats this Name before having sexual
intercourse with his wife, will be blessed by Allāh with a
righteous child.

AL-KHĀLIQ

THE CREATOR

He is Allāh, the Creator. (59 : 24)

Al-Khāliq is an Attribute of Allāh. This name is derived from the word *Khalaq* which means to produce, to make, to assign, to assess and to bring into existence from non-existence. Allāh is the only One Who has created the heavens and the earth, Who has created night, Who has created life and death, Who has created all things and beings in pairs and Who has knowledge of the nature of all the creations and exact stage of their making and production. He has divided all material and abstract things into different kinds, categories and shapes. Allāh is the One and the only Being Who will remain for ever, and in Whom all these qualities besides many other are manifested to the utmost, and He is called *Al-Khāliq*.

He who repeats this Name at night, Allāh will appoint an angel for his security and protection till the Day of Judgment. The reward for this angel's actions will be given to that person.

AL-BĀRI'
THE MAKER

اَلْبَارِئُ جَلَّ جَلَالُهُ

هُوَ اللّٰهُ الْخَالِقُ الْبَارِئُ

He is Allāh, The Creator, the Maker. (59 : 24)

Baraa implies a process of evolving from previously created matter or state : the Author of this process is *Bāri-u*, the Evolver or the Maker. Allāh is *Al-Bāri'* because He creates all things in proportion. He is the Moulder of each form and frame. He is the Designer, Builder of earth and Heavens. He has fashioned His angels and made them messengers. Verily He is Mighty. None can withhold what He bestoweth and none what He withholdeth can send.

If a woman who desires to give birth to a child, but cannot, fasts for seven days, and on each day at the time of *Iftār* repeats three Names of Allāh : *Al-Khāliq, Al-Bāri', Al-Musawwir,* twenty-one times, breathes into a cup of water and then breaks the fast with this water, Allāh will bless her with a child.

AL-MUSAWWIR
THE FASHIONER

He is Allāh, the Creator, the Maker, the Fash-ioner. (59 : 24)

Sawwara implies giving definite form or colour, so as to make a thing exactly suited to a given end or object : hence the title *Musawwir*, Bestower of Forms or colours *i.e.*, the Fashioner. Allāh is *Al-Musawwir*, because He designs all things.

If a sterile woman keeps fast for seven days, breaks her fast every evening with a drink of water over which this sacred name of Allāh has been recited twenty one times, she will be blessed with a child.

AL-GHAFFĀR
THE GREAT FORGIVER الغفار جَلَّ جَلاَلُهُ

تَدْعُونَنِى لِاَكْفُرَ بِاللهِ وَاُشْرِكَ بِهِ
مَالَيْسَ لِى بِهِ عِلْمٌ وَاَنَا اَدْعُوكُمْ
اِلَى الْعَزِيْزِ الْغَفَّارِ ۞

*Ye call me to disbelieve in Allāh and ascribe
unto Him as partners that whereof I have no
knowledge, while I call you unto the Mighty,
the Great Forgiver. (40 : 42)*

Al-Ghaffār means to cover a thing. Allāh is *Ghaffār*
because he hides the sins of His servants. It means we
people commit sins but Allāh with His Infinite mercy
forgives our faults and blunders.

In *Sahih al-Bukhāri* the following prayer is called
Sayyid al-Istaghfar :

فَقُلْتُ اسْتَغْفِرُوْا رَبَّكُمْ طِ اِنَّهُ كَانَ
غَفَّارًا ۞

*And I have said : Seek pardon of your Lord.
Lo ! He was ever Forgiving. (71 : 10)*

He who recites this Name, Allāh will forgive his sins.

AL-QAHHĀR

اَلْقَهَّارُ جَلَّ جَلَالُهُ

THE DOMINANT

قُلِ اللهُ خَالِقُ كُلِّ شَىْءٍ وَّهُوَالْوَاحِدُ الْقَهَّارُ ۵

Say: Allāh is the Creator of all things, and He is the One, the Dominant. (13 : 16)

This word is derived from *Qahhir* which means dominance. The Dominant is One Who has greater Commanding influence even on the influentials. The claim of a human being that he holds complete dominance over other human being, nation or country is absolutely false and leads to destruction. It is only Allāh Who deserves this name because He has full control over our spirit, body, movement etc. Allāh is *al-Qahhār* because He is dominant in a way that He can do anything He wills.

He who repeats this Name will control his worldly desires. He will gain spiritual contentment and inner peace. The repetition of this Name also protects one from doing evil deeds.

AL-WAHHĀB
THE BESTOWER

Our Lord! Cause not our hearts to stray after Thou hast guided us, and bestow upon us mercy from Thy Presence. Lo! Thou, only Thou, art the Bestower. (3 : 8)

Wahāb is derived from *Wahaba*. *Hibba* and *Muhib* are also derived from it. *Wahhāb* means the great and permanent Bestower. It should be remembered that *Hibba* is that donation or gift which is given without personal interest, hope and free of cost. Hadrat Ibrahim (peace be upon him) was turned out of the borders of country by the King. Allāh bestowed upon him enormous wealth in the shape of two sons Hadrat Isma'il and Hadrat Ishaq (peace be upon them). He thanked God on their birth.

Allāh is Bestower because He is the real Owner of all sorts of gifts whether visible and invisible or worldly or in the Hereafter. This name tells us that man owns nothing; whatever he owns he holds only with the munificence of Allāh.

The person who repeats this Name seven times after *Du'a* (supplication) appealing to Allāh, his appeal will be answered. A needy person, or a person who is captured by an enemy, or someone who can't earn enough to maintain himself, if he repeats this Name for three or seven nights 100 times after *two rak'ahs* of *Nafl* (Voluntary) prayer at midnight, Allāh will bless him with all his needs, and free him from the clutches of enemy.

AR-RAZZĀQ
THE PROVIDER

الرَّزَّاقُ جَلَّ جَلَالُهُ

اِنَّ اللهَ هُوَ الرَّزَّاقُ

Verily, Allāh! He is the Provider. (51 : 58)

Ar-Razzāq is an Attribute of Allāh. Its root is *Rizq*, which means foods and drinks required for the appeasement of hunger besides wealth comprising the necessities, luxuries and comforts of all sorts for the worldly life and such training and opportunities for appeasement of the spiritual urge of those people who are desirous to be fully prepared for the life after death. It has been observed that at times the parents have to bring up their children, the master has to feed his servants, the guardian has to support and help his ward and the king has to look after the welfare of his subjects. But all these arrangements and performances are purely temporary and under the direction of the Real King, Lord and Creator of all the creations, at His will and pleasure. As a sign of our gratitude for His beneficence and blessings showered on us, we must also feed the hungry people and give charity to the needy. Allāh is *Ar-Razzāq* because He provides all things beneficial to His creatures.

He who recites this Name will be provided with sustenance by Allāh.

AL-FATTĀH
THE JUDGE

الْفَتَّاحُ جَلَّ جَلَالُهُ

قُلْ يَجْمَعُ بَيْنَنَا رَبُّنَا ثُمَّ يَفْتَحُ بَيْنَنَا بِالْحَقِّ ۚ وَهُوَ الْفَتَّاحُ الْعَلِيمُ ۝

Say: Our Lord will bring us all together, then He will judge between us with truth. He is the All-Knowing Judge. (34 : 26)

Al-Fattāh is a Name of Allāh, its root being *Fath* which has two meanings *viz.*, 'Opening' and 'success', and *Miftah* means 'key'. Now let us see what are the meanings conveyed by *Al-Fattāh* according to different verses of the Holy Qur'ān. On Doomsday, truth will be opened. It will be of no avail to the unbelievers if they admit the truth on that Day, when the obedient servants of Allāh will be blessed and recompensed. In the Holy Qur'ān, this name is also combined with another name of Allāh *viz.*, *'Aleem.* It is Allāh only, Who opens the door of success for overcoming all the troubles and obstacles encountered by us, Who opens our hearts for the truth, Who makes knowledge flow from our tongues, Who unveils the accomplishments of different sciences before our eyes, Who makes the believers profess, while sins of the unbelievers are unveiled before all. We must pray to Allāh with the name *Al-Fattāh* as follows:

O' Allāh! I be to You to endow me with Your blessings of all kinds, from the beginning to the end, complete in all respects, in this worldy life as well as the life Hereafter, and grant me salvation and high ranks among the denizens of Paradise.

He who repeats this Name, Allāh will enlighten his mind and he will be given victory.

AL-'ALIM
THE ALL-KNOWING

Unto Allāh belong the East and the West, and whithersoever ye turn, there is Allāh's countenance. Lo! Allāh is All-Embracing, All-Knowing. (2:115)

Al-'Alim is an Attribute of Allāh. It belongs to the root *'Ilm* which means knowledge. In many verses of the Holy Qur'ān, this name manifests that His knowledge is complete in all respects and encompasses the knowledge of everything that exists. He has knowledge of all things hidden or manifest, whether in heaven or on earth. He knows the number of the leaves of the trees, of the grains of wheat and of sand. Events, past and future are known to Him. He knows what enters into the heart of man and what he utters with his mouth. He alone, except those to whom He has revealed them, knows the invisible things. He is free from forgetfulness, negligence and error. His knowledge is eternal; it is not posterior to His essence.

He who recites this Name, his heart will become luminous, revealing divine light *(Nūr)*.

AS-SAMI'
THE ALL-HEARING

هُنَالِكَ دَعَا زَكَرِيَّا رَبَّهُ ۚ قَالَ رَبِّ
هَبْ لِي مِن لَّدُنكَ ذُرِّيَّةً طَيِّبَةً ۖ إِنَّكَ
سَمِيعُ الدُّعَآءِ ٥

*Then Zachariah prayed unto his Lord and said:
My Lord! Bestow upon me of Thy bounty
goodly offspring. Lo! Thou art the Hearer of
Prayer.* (3 : 38)

As-Sami' is one of the famous Attributes of Allāh,
which means that He hears all sounds whether low or
loud. He hears without an ear, for His Attributes are not
like those of men. Our hearing power is limited and is in
no way comparable with His hearing power, as He hears
the speeches and sounds of all human beings, animals,
insects and all other creatures of land, water and air,
everywhere, besides those thoughts, desires and prayers in
the minds and hearts that are not uttered in words or
sounds. He is the One and the only Being Who will
remain for ever, and Who listens to all the prayers and
sounds of millions, billions, trillions, say of countless
creatures simultaneously without disruption. We must
always pray to Allāh with implicit faith that He listens to

all our prayers, as He is called *As-Sami'*, and He likes such a servant who is ever praying, pleading and begging Him for favours.

He who recites this Name 100 times without speaking to anyone on Thursdays after the *Zuhr* (Noon) Prayer, Allāh will bestow on him any desire.

AL-BASIR
THE ALL-SEEING ONE

قُلْ اَؤُنَبِّئُكُمْ بِخَيْرٍ مِّنْ ذٰلِكُمْ لِلَّذِينَ اتَّقَوْا عِنْدَ رَبِّهِمْ جَنّٰتٌ تَجْرِى مِنْ تَحْتِهَا الْاَنْهٰرُ خٰلِدِينَ فِيهَا وَ اَزْوَاجٌ مُّطَهَّرَةٌ وَّرِضْوَانٌ مِّنَ اللّٰهِ وَاللّٰهُ بَصِيْرٌ بِالْعِبَادِ ۟

Say : Shall I inform you of something better than that? For those who keep from evil, with their Lord are Garden underneath which rivers flow, and pure companions, and contentment from Allāh: Allāh is Seer of His bondmen. (3 : 15)

Al-Basir is a Name of Allāh from the root *Basar*, which means the ability of seeing. He sees all things, even the steps of a black ant on a black stone in a dark night; yet He has no eye as men have. He is aware of the conditions of His servants, their deeds and all matters. He has created the powers of hearing and seeing for us, but these are not like His powers, which are beyond our thinking capacity. He sees, feels and reads in the past, present and future, in the hearts and minds, in the depths of oceans and the darkness of nights, nothing is hidden or kept secret from Him. The best course is that we should bow down before Him with purity of thought and implicit faith, submitting ourselves entirely at His will and pleasure, as He is called *al-Basir*.

He who repeats this Name 100 times between first four *rak'ahs* of *Sunnah* and *Fard* prayer at *Jum'a*, Allāh will give this person esteem in the eyes of others.

AL-LAṬIF
THE SUBTLE ONE

اللَّطِيف جَلَّ جَلَالُهُ

لَا تُدْرِكُهُ الْاَبْصَارُ وَهُوَ يُدْرِكُ
الْاَبْصَارَ وَهُوَ اللَّطِيفُ الْخَبِيرُه

Vision comprehendeth Him not, but He comprehendeth (all) vision. He is the Subtle One, the Aware. (6 : 103)

Al-Latif, as a Name of Allāh, is as difficult to define in words as the idea it seeks to represent is difficult to grasp in our minds. It implies :

1. Fine, Subtle (the basic meaning);
2. So Fine and Subtle as to be imperceptible to human sight;
3. So pure as to be incomprehensible;
4. With sight so perfect as to see and understand the finest subtleties and mysteries;
5. So Kind and Gracious as to bestow gifts of the most refined kind; extraordinarily gracious and understanding.

Allah is *Al-Latif* because He knows the delicate meanings of everything. Allāh is *Al-Latif* because He creates things most subtly, which cannot be understood by people. Allāh is *Al-Latif* because He gives blessings to people in the most subtle ways.

He who has become poor, and is also helpless, if he repeats this Name 100 times after two *rak'ahs* of *Nafl* (Voluntary) prayer, his desires will be fulfilled.

AL-KHABIR
THE AWARE

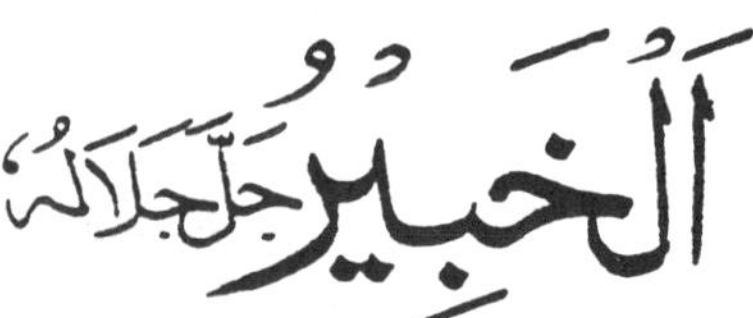

اَلْحَمْدُ لِلّٰهِ الَّذِى لَهُ مَا فِى السَّمٰوٰتِ وَمَا فِى الْاَرْضِ وَلَهُ الْحَمْدُ فِى الْاٰخِرَةِ ۭ وَ هُوَ الْحَكِيْمُ الْخَبِيْرُ ۰

Praise be to Allāh, unto Whom belongeth whatsoever is in the heavens and whatsoever is in the earth. His is the praise in the Hereafter, and He is the Wise, the Aware. (34 : 1)

Al-Khabir is a Name of Allāh having two roots *Khabar* and *Khaburat i.e.,* Allāh, the Omniscient knows, witnesses and sees all things and is aware of all conditions anywhere, hidden, invisible or visible, all news of this world and the world of Hereafter. In the Holy Qur'ān, this name *al-Khabir* has appeared with some other names of Allāh *i.e., al-Hakim, al-'Alim* etc. The name of *al-Khabir* implies that the information about all actions of the others is in His knowledge. He knows, hears and sees all our good and evil intentions and deeds, and warned of punishments for the vicious and sinful acts. We are answerable to Him for everything we think of, say or do, hence we must be true, righteous and sincere in our faith, intentions and acts. While praying to Him with the name of *al-Khabir*, we must try to find out the needs of the poor and meek persons and help them as far as possible.

He who has a bad habit and desires to get rid of it, if he repeats this Name continuously, will be quickly freed from this habit by the grace of Allāh.

AL-ḤALĪM
THE CLEMENT

الحليم جلّ جلاله

تُسَبِّحُ لَهُ السَّمٰوٰتُ السَّبْعُ وَالْاَرْضُ وَمَنْ فِيهِنَّ ط وَاِنْ مِّنْ شَىْءٍ اِلَّا يُسَبِّحُ بِحَمْدِهٖ وَلٰكِنْ لَّا تَفْقَهُوْنَ تَسْبِيْحَهُمْ ط اِنَّهٗ كَانَ حَلِيْمًا غَفُوْرًا ٥

The seven heavens and the earth and all that is therein praise Him, and there is not a thing but hymneth His praise; but ye understand not their praise. Lo! He is ever Clement, Forgiving.
(17 : 44)

Al-Halim is a Name of Allāh from *Hilm*, which means tolerance, forbearance, serenity, affability, wisdom etc. It implies that Allāh Who is called *al-Halim* is never in a hurry to punish His servants for their sins and gives them ample time to repent and make amends. His mercy overcomes His anger and He is ever inclined to forgive on penitence. Allāh praised and appreciated the forbearance of Hadrat Isma'il (peace be upon him) and called him *Halim* because on hearing of the horrifying news that he was to be sacrificed at the commands of Allāh he was as serene and calm as before. While praying to Him with this name *al-Halim*, we must be tolerant, forbearing and affable in our treatment and dealings with everybody, friend or foe. If we hear that somebody is falsely accusing and slandering us, we must wait with patience for the results and justice of Allāh, Who has complete knowledge of everything.

If one writes this Name on a piece of paper, and puts it in the place where seed is sown, no harm, disaster or calamity will befall his crop.

AL-'AZĪM
THE GREAT ONE

اَللهُ لَاۤ اِلٰهَ اِلَّا هُوَ ۚ اَلْحَىُّ الْقَيُّوْمُ ۚ لَا تَأْخُذُهُ سِنَةٌ وَّلَا نَوْمٌ ۚ لَهُ مَا فِى السَّمٰوٰتِ وَمَا فِى الْاَرْضِ ۗ مَنْ ذَا الَّذِىْ يَشْفَعُ عِنْدَهٗۤ اِلَّا بِاِذْنِهٖ ۚ يَعْلَمُ مَا بَيْنَ اَيْدِيْهِمْ وَمَا خَلْفَهُمْ ۚ وَلَا يُحِيْطُوْنَ بِشَىْءٍ مِّنْ عِلْمِهٖۤ اِلَّا بِمَا شَآءَ ۚ وَسِعَ كُرْسِيُّهُ السَّمٰوٰتِ وَالْاَرْضَ ۚ وَلَا يَـُٔوْدُهٗ حِفْظُهُمَا ۚ وَهُوَ الْعَلِىُّ الْعَظِيْمُ ۝

Allāh! There is no god save Him, the Ever-Living, the Eternal. Neither slumber nor sleep overtaketh Him. Unto Him belongeth whatsoever is in the heavens and whatsoever is on the earth. Who is he that intercedeth with Him except by His permission? He knoweth that which is in front of them and that which is behind them, while they encompass nothing of His knowledge save what He willeth. His

*Throne overspreads the heavens and the earth,
and the guarding of them wearies Him not.
And He is the Sublime and the Great.* (2 : 255)

Allāh is called *al-'Azim* as He is above everything in Divinity, and also as He is the One and the only Being, Who will remain for ever. There is no god save Him, the Ever-Living, the Eternal. He is the Creator of the great heavens, the Most Bounteous, the Greatest of all. Unto Him belongeth whatsoever is in the heavens and whatsoever is on the earth. His Throne overspreads the heavens and the earth. He is the Maker of kings, the Saviour of all beings from trials and tribulations, and He gives honour and power to whom He likes. He has bestowed the Holy Qur'ān on His servants for their guidance and salvation. He brings all the creations into existence from non-existence. He guides His obedient servants to success and salvation in the eternal life. While praying to Him with the name *al-'Azim* there should be no trace of thoughts in our minds about greatness of any materials or creations.

He who repeats this Name many times will be respected by others.

AL-GHAFŪR
THE ALL-FORGIVING الغفورجلّجلاله

وَمِنَ النَّاسِ وَالدَّوَآبِّ وَالْاَنْعَامِ مُخْتَلِفٌ اَلْوَانُهٗ كَذٰلِكَ ۗ اِنَّمَا يَخْشَى اللّٰهَ مِنْ عِبَادِهِ الْعُلَمٰٓؤُاْ ۗ اِنَّ اللّٰهَ عَزِيْزٌ غَفُوْرٌ ۟

And of men and beasts and cattle, in like manner, divers hues? The erudite among His bondsmen fear Allāh alone. Lo! Allāh is Mighty, Forgiving. (35 : 28)

Al-Ghafūr is an Attribute of Allāh. The name *al-Ghafūr* denotes forgiving of sins and making the sinners forget their sins so that no trace of the feeling of regret remains in their memory. Salvation is there from Allah for His servants as He is called *al-Ghafūr*. He accepts gratitude and has affection for all. He is most merciful to His meek and humble servants. While praying to Him with this name *al-Ghafūr*, we must try to recollect our countless sins and beg pardon for them with implicit faith and belief that He is the Most Merciful and will forgive us and wash out our sins. It must be remembered that this name *al-Ghafūr* while denoting the pardon of sins is not at all encouraging for sinful future, rather it makes us ashamed of our sins and warns us against their repetition in future.

Allāh is Oft-Forgiving, Most Merciful. Even when we suffer trials and tribulations, it is for our good, and no one can remove them except He, when in His plan He sees it to be best for all concerned. On the other hand, there is no power that can intercept His blessings and favours, and His bounty flows freely when we are worthy, and often when we are not worthy of it.

He who has a headache, or is suffering from fever, or is despondent, if he repeats this Name continuously, will be relieved of his ailment.

ASH-SHAKŪR 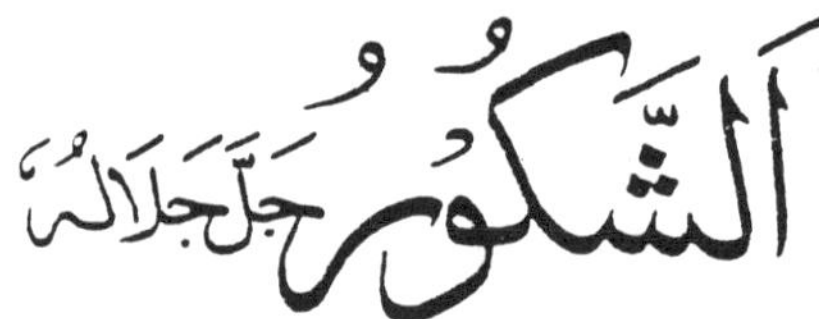
THE APPRECIATIVE

That He will pay them their wages and increase them of His grace. Lo! He is Forgiving, Appreciative. (35 : 30)

And they say : Praise be to Allāh Who hath put grief away from us. Lo! Our Lord is Forgiving, Bountiful. (35 : 34)

Shakūr like *Shakir* when applied to Allāh means One Who highly appreciates good deeds and is Bountiful in rewarding them. Allāh is *Shakūr* because He appreciates and recognises any good deed, however little, which He finds in us and gives us a reward beyond all measures. Allāh is *Ash-Shakūr* because He is bountiful and gives reward for deeds done for Him.

He who has a heavy heart, and repeats this Name 41 times over a glass of water, then washes his face with this water, his heart will lighten, and he will be able to maintain himself.

AL-'ALIYY

THE SUBLIME

Unto Him belongeth all that is in the Heavens and all that is in the earth, and He is the Sublime, the Tremendous. (42 : 4)

Al-'Aliyy is a Name of Allāh coming from *'Aluv'* which means 'eminence', 'greatness', 'supremacy', 'grandeur' and 'loftiness'. He is called *al-'Aliyy* as He is Sublime and Omnipotent; as He is Lofty and Eminent; as He is above all evils and vices; as He is Wise, Superior and above everything in Divinity. He reserved superiority and high ranks for His most obedient and selected servants. He elevated Hadrat Idris (peace be upon him) to eminent position. His name is *al-'Aliyy*, His command is Supreme. He is Most High and Mighty. In our prayers and at all times, we must remember again and again His greatness and supremacy, and we must act with courage and spirit in all matters, bowing humbly only before Him for favours and blessings.

He whose faith is weak and repeats this Name, his faith will become sound and right and he will reach his destination.

AL-KABIR
THE MOST GREAT

وَلَا تَنْفَعُ الشَّفَاعَةُ عِنْدَهُ إِلَّا لِمَنْ
اَذِنَ لَهُ ۚ حَتَّى إِذَا فُزِّعَ عَنْ قُلُوبِهِمْ
قَالُوا مَاذَا ۙ قَالَ رَبُّكُمْ ۖ قَالُوا الْحَقَّ
وَهُوَ الْعَلِيُّ الْكَبِيرُ ۝

No intercession availeth with Him save for him whom He permitteth. Yet, when fear is banished from their hearts, they say: What was it that your Lord said? They say: The Truth. And He is the Sublime, the Most Great. (34 : 23)

Al-Kabir is a Name of Allāh coming from *Kibr* which means greatness, haughtiness, pride and dignity. It implies that He is Most Dignified and Greatest. He is the One and the Only Being, Whose existence is free of time and place. He is existing from Eternity and will remain for ever to Eternity. He is the Creator and Sustainer of all creations, worlds, heavens and earth including all those places which were shown to the Holy Prophet Muhammad (peace and blessings of Allāh be upon him). He knows all things, acts and facts open or hidden anywhere, and He is Lofty and above everything in Divinity. His grandeur and greatness will be shown on the Great Day, when He will shower immense blessings on

His obedient servants, and they will be rewarded profusely. He is pure and free of all evils, vices, defects, sexes, blemishes and necessities. The Holy Prophet Muhammad (peace and blessings of Allāh be upon him) has prescribed the following prayer for our recitation :

O' Allāh! make me small in my own eyes and great in the eyes of other people.

He who repeats this Name 100 times daily will become honourable and respectable in the eyes of the world.

AL-HAFIZ

THE PRESERVER

فَاِنْ تَوَلَّوْا فَقَدْ اَبْلَغْتُكُمْ مَّا اُرْسِلْتُ بِهٖٓ اِلَيْكُمْ ۫ وَيَسْتَخْلِفُ رَبِّيْ قَوْمًا غَيْرَكُمْ ۚ وَلَا تَضُرُّوْنَهٗ شَيْئًا ۭ اِنَّ رَبِّيْ عَلٰى كُلِّ شَيْءٍ حَفِيْظٌ ۞

And if ye turn away, still I have conveyed unto you that wherewith I was sent unto you, and my Lord will set in place of you a folk other than you. Ye cannot injure Him at all. Lo! my Lord is Guardian over all things. (11 : 57)

Al-Hafiz is a Name of Allāh denoting the meanings 'guarding', 'watching', 'protecting', 'custody' and 'preserving'. He is called *al-Hafiz*, as He is the custodian of all creations and existing things. He is the Guardian and Protector of all beings from calamities, catastrophes, disasters, troubles and sufferings. He has erected the sky in space without pillars and likewise the earth without foundation, along with sun, the moon and the stars, all operating under His care, and for all this care, custody and guardianship He is never tired and slack. He is the Omnipotent Being, free from any weaknesses and defects. It is Allāh only Who assigns angels for ptotecting us from evils, Who defeats the evil designs of *Satan* against us, Who safeguards the chastity of His obedient womenfolk, Who has bestowed on us the Holy Book which contains guidance for us. It is Allāh only Who protects us against all evils and calamities. Praying to Him with this name *Al-Hafiz*, we must keep aloof from evil thoughts and deeds and ignore worldly protective devices and security measures, having implicit faith and trust in Him for protection and safety of our life, property and family from all troubles and calamities, bowing down before Him for guidance and subjecting ourselves entirely to His will and pleasure.

He who repeats this Name 16 times each day, Allāh will protect him from calamities.

AL-MUQĪT
THE MAINTAINER

المقيت جَلَّ جَلالُه

من يَشْفَعْ شَفَاعَةً حَسَنَةً يَكُنْ لَّهُ نَصِيبٌ مِّنْهَا ۚ وَمَن يَشْفَعْ شَفَاعَةً سَيِّئَةً يَكُن لَّهُ كِفْلٌ مِّنْهَا ۗ وَكَانَ اللّهُ عَلَى كُلِّ شَيْءٍ مُّقِيتًا ٥

Whoso interveneth in a good cause will have the reward thereof, and whoso interveneth in an evil cause will bear the consequence thereof. Allāh overseeth all things. (4 : 85)

Al-Muqīt is an Attribute of Allāh which means "the Guardian". Allāh is called *al-Muqīt* because He is the sustainer of all creations. Praying to Allāh with this name *al-Muqīt*, we must solicit His blessings and favours for sustaining, increasing and improving our physical, intellectual and spiritual powers and endowing us with the will and determination to devote all these powers in the performance of duties entrusted to us by Him.

If a person having a bad-mannered child repeats this Name over a glass of water, and gives this water to the child to drink, the child will have good manners.

AL-HASIB
THE RECKONER الحسيب جَلَّ جَلَالُه

وَمَنْ كَانَ غَنِيًّا فَلْيَسْتَعْفِفْ وَمَنْ كَانَ
فَقِيرًا فَلْيَأْكُلْ بِالْمَعْرُوفِ فَإِذَا دَفَعْتُمْ
إِلَيْهِمْ أَمْوَالَهُمْ فَأَشْهِدُوا عَلَيْهِمْ
وَكَفَى بِاللهِ حَسِيبًا

Whoso (of the guardians) is rich, let him abstain generously (from taking of the property of orphans); and whoso is poor, let him take thereof in reason (for his guardianship). And when ye deliver up their fortune unto orphans, have (the transaction) witnessed in their presence. Allāh sufficeth as a Reckoner. (4 : 6)

Al-Hasib is an Attribute of Allāh which means "the Reckoner" on the Day of Judgment. This title occurs in the Holy Qur'ān three times. All our virtuous deeds and sins will be reckoned by Him on the Day of Judgment and we will be rewarded or punished accordingly. Blessings and favours for His obedient servants will be enormous and countless. Allāh is *Al-Hasib* because He knows in detail the account of deeds people do throughout their lives.

If one is afraid of being robbed, or is afraid of the jealousy of an Envious, or is afraid of being harmed or wronged, he may begin on a Thursday to repeat this Name. 70 times day and night for seven days and at the seventy first time say "Allāh is my Reckoner" (*Hasbiy-allāh-ul-Hasib*), he will be free of his fears if God, Most High, willeth.

AL-KARIM
THE GENEROUS ONE

يَا أَيُّهَا الْإِنْسَانُ مَا غَرَّكَ بِرَبِّكَ الْكَرِيمِ

O' man! What hath made thee careless concerning thy Lord, the Generous One. (82 : 6)

Al-Karim is one of the ninety-nine Attributes of Allāh which means "the Generous One". He is really bounteous because He sent the Holy Prophet Muhammad (peace and blessings of Allāh be upon him) and also revealed through him the Holy Qur'ān for our guidance and salvation. He rewards His obedient servants profusely and will admit them to Paradise by His command. He is the most bountiful because He sustains all the creations and provides them food and all other necessities of life. Allāh is Just as well as Generous. To the good the reward is multiplied ten times (*i.e.,* far above merits) on account of His generosity. To the evil, the punishment is no more than commensurate with their sin, and even so the door of mercy is always open to those who sincerely repent and show it by their conduct.

He who recites this Name many times will have esteem in this world and in the Hereafter.

AR-RAQIB
THE WATCHFUL

الرَّقِيب جَلَّ جَلَالُه

يَا أَيُّهَا النَّاسُ اتَّقُوا رَبَّكُمُ الَّذِى خَلَقَكُمْ مِنْ نَفْسٍ وَّاحِدَةٍ وَّخَلَقَ مِنْهَا زَوْجَهَا وَبَثَّ مِنْهُمَا رِجَالًا كَثِيْرًا وَّنِسَاءً ۚ وَاتَّقُوا اللهَ الَّذِى تَسَاءَلُوْنَ بِهِ وَالْأَرْحَامَ ۚ إِنَّ اللهَ كَانَ عَلَيْكُمْ رَقِيْبًاه

O' mankind! Be careful of your duty to your Lord Who created you from a single soul and from it created its mate and from them twain hath spread abroad a multitude of men and women. Be careful of your duty toward Allāh in Whom ye claim (your rights) of one another, and toward the wombs (that bear you). Lo! Allāh hath been a Watcher over you. (4 : 1)

Ar-Raqib is one of the ninety-nine Attributes of Almighty, which means "the Watchful". He observes all creatures, and every action is under His control. It is Allāh only Who keeps watch over all creations and protects us from all evils and calamities. Praying to Him with this name Ar-Raqib, we must entrust Him with all our affairs and try to mould our lives as directed by Him in the Holy Qur'ān and further elaborated in the traditions of the Holy Prophet Muhammad (peace and blessings of Allāh be upon him) which is the only way to secure ourselves from the evil designs of *Satan*. Allāh watches over us and guards us, and provides all kinds of agencies, material, moral and spiritual, to help our growth and development, keep us from harm and bring us nearer to our Destiny.

He who repeats this Name seven times over himself, his family and his property, all will be under the protection of Allāh.

AL-QARIB
THE NIGH

وَاِلٰى ثَمُودَ اَخَاهُمْ صٰلِحًا قَالَ يٰقَوْمِ اعْبُدُوا اللّٰهَ مَا لَكُمْ مِنْ اِلٰهٍ غَيْرُهُ هُوَ اَنْشَاَكُمْ مِنَ الْاَرْضِ وَاسْتَعْمَرَكُمْ فِيهَا فَاسْتَغْفِرُوهُ ثُمَّ تُوبُوا اِلَيْهِ اِنَّ رَبِّى قَرِيبٌ مُّجِيبٌ ۰

And unto (the tribe of) Thamud (We sent) their borther Salih. He said: O' my people! Serve Allāh, ye have no other god save Him. He brought you forth from the earth and hath made you husband it. So ask forgiveness of Him and turn unto Him repentant. Lo! my Lord is Nigh, Responsive. (11 : 61)

Al-Qarib is an Attribute of Allāh which means "Allāh is near at hand". So one can invoke His help directly without the help of an interceder. Though He is the Highest, each one of you will find Him so near yourself that you will be able to convey your request even in a whisper, nay, you are permitted to convey your requests openly or secretly to Him. Therefore give up the folly of seeking interceders and setting them up as His partners, and address your prayers to Him Who is near at hand and answers prayers. Though we cannot see Him and feel Him with our senses, we must never imagine that He is far from us. Nay, He is so near to every servant that we can invoke Him and place our requests before Him wherever we may be. So much so that He hears and answers even those requests which are not expressed in words but are made only in the innermost heart.

AL-MUJIB
THE RESPONSIVE

ٱلْمُجِيبُ جَلَّ جَلَالُهُ

وَاِلٰى ثَمُودَ اَخَاهُمْ صٰلِحًا ۘ قَالَ يٰقَوْمِ اعْبُدُوا اللّٰهَ مَا لَكُمْ مِّنْ اِلٰهٍ غَيْرُهٗ ؕ هُوَ اَنْشَاَكُمْ مِّنَ الْاَرْضِ وَاسْتَعْمَرَكُمْ فِيْهَا فَاسْتَغْفِرُوْهُ ثُمَّ تُوْبُوْٓا اِلَيْهِ ؕ اِنَّ رَبِّيْ قَرِيْبٌ مُّجِيْبٌ ۠

And unto (the tribe of) Thamud (We sent) their brother Salih. He said: O' my people! Serve Allāh, ye have no other god save Him. He brought you forth from the earth and hath made you husband it. So ask forgiveness of Him and turn unto Him repentant. Lo! my Lord is Nigh, Responsive. (11 : 116)

Al-Mujib is an Attribute of Allāh which means the "One Who answers to" (a prayer). Allāh is the One Who responds to every need. When anyone prays to Allāh and wants something from Him, He answers to his prayer and fulfils his needs. We must have implicit faith in Him and must always act in obedience to His Commands, praying with the firm belief that He will certainly accept our prayers. Allāh is *Al-Mujib* because He biddest men to pray and hearest their prayers.

He who repeats this Name, his appeal will be answered.

AL-WĀSIʿ
THE ALL-EMBRACING

Allāh bestoweth His sovereignty on whom He will: Allāh is All-Embracing, All-Knowing. (2 : 247)

Wāsiʿ is a name of Allāh that manifests His greatness, munificence, power and might. This name denotes that His generosity, and magnanimity are beyond limits and estimates rather beyond imagination. His bounties encompass all creatures and things, and the vastness of His Knowledge is far more than the entire expanse of the earth and the heavens. He is indeed Powerful and Mighty. The specific invocation with reference to this name of Allāh is as follows:

O' Allāh! We cannot see you nor think and imagine, nor is it in our power to offer sufficient praises and gratitude for your munificence and the bounties showered on us. Particularly we solicit more of Your favours in the old age.

If one who has difficulty in earning his livelihood, repeats this Name, his income will be increased if God, the Most High,.willeth.

AL-HAKIM

THE WISE

Our Lord! And raise up in their midst a messenger from among them who shall recite unto them Thy revelations, and shall instruct them in the Scripture and in wisdom and shall make them grow. Lo! Thou, only Thou, art the Mighty, Wise. (2 : 129)

Al-Hakim is a name of Allāh. According to majority of the distinguished Muslim Scholars it manifests His *Hikma* which carries multifarious meanings, effects and purposes. It means the knowledge of right acts and deeds. It covers the laudable objects and purposes connected with the creation of all things as well as the expediencies of the system of control of the Universe. Its intrinsic meaning is to determine excellent things by Supreme Knowledge and Wisdom. He is *Ḥakim* and bestows *Hikma* i.e., wisdom on whomsoever He wills.

Thos name of Allāh *Hakim* has appeared alongside

another name *'Aziz* in 24 contexts in the Holy Qur'ān, and it has also appeared with more of the other names *Viz . Hameed, Khabeer, Wāsi'* and *'Aleem*, with the object of amplifying the meanings. In order to ascertain the intrinsic meanings and beneficial effects of the recital of this name of Allāh, We must acquire knowledge and understanding of the Holy Qur'ān and the *Ahadith* (Traditions) of the Messenger of Allāh (peace and blessings of Allāh be upon him).

He who recites this Name from time to time will not have difficulties in his work.

AL-WADUD
THE LOVING

وَاسْتَغْفِرُوا رَبَّكُمْ ثُمَّ تُوبُوا اِلَيْهِ
اِنَّ رَبِّى رَحِيمٌ وَّدُودٌ ۝

Ask pardon of your Lord and then turn unto Him (repentant). Lo! my Lord is Merciful, Loving. (11 : 90)

Wadūd is another Attribute of Allāh. It means that Entity which is loved, adored and worshipped. His obedient servants love Him and He loves them. Undoubtedly, love is from both sides. It is initiated by Allāh and reciprocated by His servants. Among the Christians, there is a saying: God is love personified. They are justifiably proud of it. But His name *Wadūd* denotes a much higher, rather incomparable and superlative degree of love. This category of love may be defined briefly as follows:

It is the permanent love from heart and soul.
It is the love in which all the dearest things are sacrificed for the beloved.
It is the love in which there is no claim for compensation.
It is the love in which all desires are annihilated.
It is the love which is unaffected by kindness or cruelty, respect or disrespect.

It is the love which denotes obedience, slavery and negation of self.

Allāh is *Al-Wadūd* because He loves those who do good and bestows on them His compassion. Allāh is the Only One Who should be loved and Whose friendship is to be earned.

If there is any dispute between two persons, and one of them repeats this Name 1,000 times over some food and gives it to the other to eat, the disagreement and unpleasantness between them will come to an end.

AL-MAJID

THE MOST GLORIOUS ONE

قَالُوٓا اَتَعْجَبِيْنَ مِنْ اَمْرِ اللّٰهِ رَحْمَتُ اللّٰهِ وَبَرَكٰتُهٗ عَلَيْكُمْ اَهْلَ الْبَيْتِ اِنَّهٗ حَمِيْدٌ مَّجِيْدٌ ۝

*They said: Wonderest thou at the Command-
ment of Allāh? The mercy of Allāh and His
blessings be upon you, O' people of the house!
Lo! He is Owner of Praise, Owner of Glory!*
(11 : 73)

Majid is a Name of Allāh, appearing in *Sura Hud* that
denotes honour, rank, dignity, glory, nobility, eminence
and excellence. It is also used as an affix with the Holy
Qur'ān. These Attributes of Allāh manifested to the
superlative degree *Majid*, are quite different and distincti-
ve from the worldly qualities. He is the Creator and Lord
of Empyrean and all the creations. His name *Majid* also
covers the other names of Allāh *viz*, *Jalil*, *Wahāb* and
Karim.

He who repeats this Name, will live in this world
honourably.

ASH-SHAHID
THE WITNESS

مَاۤ اَصَابَكَ مِنْ حَسَنَةٍ فَمِنَ اللهِ وَمَاۤ اَصَابَكَ مِنْ سَيِّئَةٍ فَمِنْ نَفْسِكَ ۚ وَ اَرْسَلْنٰكَ لِلنَّاسِ رَسُوْلًا ۚ وَكَفٰى بِاللهِ شَهِيْدًا ۝

Whatever of good befalleth thee (O' man) it is from Allāh, and whatever of ill befalleth thee it is from thyself. We have sent thee (Muhammad) as a messenger unto mankind and Allāh is sufficient as Witness. (4 : 79)

Shahid is a Name of Allāh originating from *Shahadat*, the meanings of which are command, administration of justice, knowledge, news, statement etc. Allāh witnesses about Himself that He is the Only One to be worhipped and none else, and that He is All Powerful and All Wise. As a faithful believer, you should uphold the cause of justice, and if called for, should witness for Allāh to establish truth, even if your evidence goes against you. Allāh is called *Shahid* because He is Omnipresent, sees and knows everything, and not a single thing or move-ment of anyone is out of His knowledge and control. The people who call and pray to Allāh with this name should remember that He sees and knows everything, and therefore, they must not lie when they bear witness. Allāh is *Ash-Shahid* because He is present everywhere and observes all things.

If a person having a rebellious and disobedient child repeats this Name, his child will become obedient.

AL-HAQQ
THE TRUTH

ذٰلِكَ بِاَنَّ اللهَ هُوَالْحَقُّ وَاَنَّهُ يُحْي الْمَوْتٰى وَاَنَّهُ عَلٰى كُلِّ شَىْءٍ قَدِيرٌ ۟

This is so because Allāh is the Truth. He brings the dead to life and He has power over everything. (22 : 6)

Allāh is the Truth. *Haqq* is one of the most significant names of Allāh. On examination of the Qur'ānic Verses, it is observed that this word has been used 227 times in the Holy Qur'ān. Its frequent use in the Holy Qur'ān shows that it is the mainstay in fulfilment of the main objectives of revelation of the Qur'ān such as to establish truth and also to teach and propagate it. No doubt Qur'ān is truth in its entirety.

The literary meanings of *Haqq* are many and varied, the most important being to speak and act upon truth. The promises of Allāh are true. The Day of Judgment is sure to come and on that Day virtuous and evil deeds of all people will be judged. The right path has been marked out for us in the Holy Qur'ān. The Messenger of Allāh (peace and blessings of Allāh be upon him) has brought truth to us. Allāh has truly created the Heavens and the

Earth. The Holy Qur'ān has been revealed with truth and it will lead us on the right path. In accordance with the many meanings and amplifications of the word *Haqq*, it is established that individually and collectively one of the most important and significant names of Allāh is *Ḥaqq*. It is Allāh only, Who reveals truth and nullifies falsehood; Who calls people to His religion Islam; Who gives glad tidings of the Hereafter; Who does and shall administer justice with truth. We must believe in the truths, search for them, demand and call for them. People wander about in East and West in search of truth, but they will not find it anywhere except in the teachings of Prophet Muhammad (peace and blessings of Allāh be upon him).

If we worship anything other than Allāh (whether it is idols, stars, powers of nature, spirits, or deified men, or Self, or Power, or Wealth, Science or Art, Talent or Intellect), our worship is both foolish and futile. Worship and prayer are justified only to the One True God.

If one has lost something and repeats this Name, he will find what is lost.

AL-WAKIL
THE TRUSTEE

فَأَعْرِضْ عَنْهُمْ وَتَوَكَّلْ عَلَى اللهِ ۚ وَكَفَىٰ بِاللهِ وَكِيلًا ۝

So oppose them and put trust in Allāh. Allāh is Sufficient as Trustee. (4:81)

Al-Wakil is a Name of Allāh that manifests His attribute as a Trustee. He has full powers and complete control over everything. There are blessings from Allāh and His Prophet for those who place confidence in Allāh and rely on Him at all times and under all circumstances. They are rewarded and raised to high ranks in this world as well as in the Hereafter. A believer must look to Him only for help and guidance, rely on Him and trust Him. So did Prophet Nuh (peace be upon him) and Prophet Ya'qub (peace be upon him) in times of trials and tribulations. Allāh is called *al-Wakil* because He provides a means to solve all problems in the best way.

Ibn 'Abbās (Allāh be pleased with him) used to say: "O' Allāh, it is unto Thee that I surrender myself, I affirm my faith in Thee and repose my trust in Thee and turn to Thee in repentance and with Thy help fought my adversaries. O' Allāh, I seek refuge in Thee with Thine Power; there is no god but Thou, lest Thou leadest me astray.

Thou art Ever - living that dieth not, while the *Jinn* and mankind die." (*Muslim*)

He who is afraid of frowning in water, or being burnt in a fire, or any similar danger, and repeats this Name from time to time, will be under the protection of Allāh.

AL-QAWI
THE MOST STRONG

اَلْقَوِىُّ جَلَّ جَلَالُه

مَا قَدَرُوا اللهَ حَقَّ قَدْرِهِ ۗ اِنَّ اللهَ لَقَوِىٌّ عَزِيزٌ ۝

They measure not Allāh His rightful measure.
Lo! Allāh is Most Strong, Almighty. (22 : 74)

Al-Qawi is an Attribute of Allāh which manifests His power. He is All-Powerful, and all powers originate from Him. He bestows powers on His creatures according to their capacities. The weak becomes strong by His Grace. The power for protection from evil also comes to the people from Allāh Who is called *al-Qawi*. He infuses faith into the hearts of believers and endows their bodies and souls with all sorts of physical and spiritual powers to perform their duties and protect themselves from mischief.

He who cannot defeat his enemy, and repeats this Name with the intention of not being harmed, his enemy will not overcome him if God, the Most High, willeth.

AL-MATIN
THE FIRM ONE

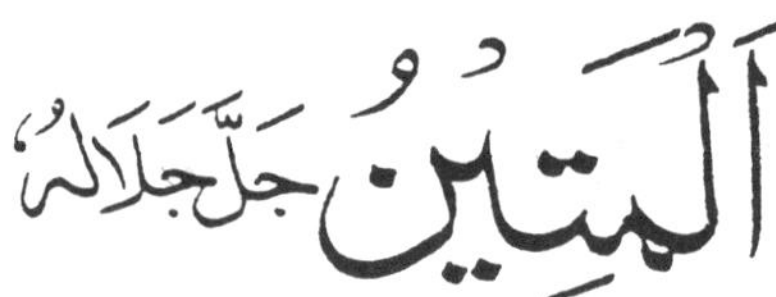

اِنَّ اللّٰهَ هُوَ الرَّزَّاقُ ذُو الْقُوَّةِ الْمَتِيْنُ ۞

Verily, Allāh! He is the Provider, the Firm One.
(51 : 58)

Al-Matin is another Attribute of Allāh, from which it is understood that He is that Almighty Being Who controls the entire Universe and all other creations without any exertion or effort. He is All-Powerful, and He Alone has the powers to provide food and other means of livelihood for all the creatures, and He has untiring and unlimited powers. *Matin* is His name, because He is Eternal and shall remain for ever. He is not dependent on anyone for anything. All the stability, reliability, strength and power are established and organised by His Command.

If one has troubles and repeats this Name, his troubles will disappear if God, the Most High, willeth.

AL-WALI

THE PROTECTING FRIEND

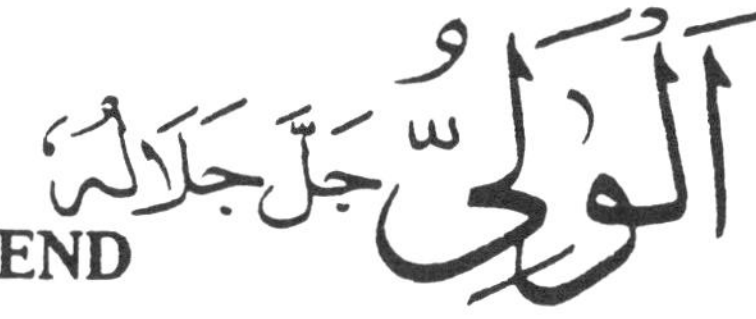

Allāh is the Protecting Friend of those who believe. (2 : 257)

Al-Wali is an Attribute of Allāh which manifests love, nearness and guardianship. Allāh is called *Wali* because. He loves, helps, protects, safeguards, guides, blesses and rewards all His faithful servants. One should offer praises and gratitude to Him and solicit His favours and help in all the problems of this world and for salvation in the Hereafter. One should not be disappointed. At His behest, justice is administered to all irrespective of their status. The poor and distressed are helped and protected by Him against any impending mischief and harm from any quarter. He is more affectionate and near to us than any of our dearest and nearest friends and relations. He is the only Protecting Friend (*Wali*) in the real sense for one and all.

He who repeats this Name is likely to be a *waliullah*, the friend of Allāh.

AL-HAMID

THE PRAISEWORTHY

الحميد جلّ جلاله

لَهُ مَا فِى السَّمٰوٰتِ وَمَا فِى الْاَرْضِ
وَاِنَّ اللهَ لَهُوَ الْغَنِىُّ الْحَمِيْدُه

*Unto Him belongeth all that is in the Heavens,
and all that is in the Earth. Lo! Allāh, He verily
is the Absolute, the Praiseworthy.* (22 : 64)

Al-Hamid is an Attribute of Allāh which means the
Praiseworthy. We must praise and love Him, offer Him
gratitude, adore and worship Him with sincerity, purity
and entirety of our heart and soul. There is the glad
tidings of recompense and rewards for His faithful servants
in this world as well as in the Hereafter. He is the Creator,
Controller and Sustainer of all the creations, and He is
the Most Beneficent and Merciful. All praises, merits,
virtues originate from Him. Allāh is called *al-Hamid* because He is the Only One to be praised and glorified and
thanked by all creatures.

He who repeats this Name will be loved and respected by the world.

AL-HAYY
THE ALIVE

Allāh! There is no god save Him, the Alive.
(3 : 2)

Al-Hayy is an Attribute of Allāh which means the Ever-living, the Deathless, the Eternal. His existence having neither beginning nor end.

Even a fact so patent as the deathlessness of God has needed a clear affirmation in view of the peculiar sacrifice of heathen gods every spring, as also in view of the "Christ-God" who suffered death at the hands of persecutors. The putting to death of a public mangod was a common incident of many religions. (*Allen* op. cit. 90)

Allāh is the only One Who is Eternal and shall remain for ever. He knows, hears and sees all our good and evil intentions and deeds, and warned of punishments for the vicious and sinful acts. We are answerable to Him for everything we think of, say or do, hence we must be true, righteous and sincere in our faith, intentions and acts.

God Most High is alone to be adored. He has neither associate nor equal. He is free from the imperfections of humanity. He is neither begotten nor does He beget. He is invisible. He is without figure, form, colour or parts. His existence has neither beginning nor end. He is immutable. If He so wills, He can annihilate the world in a moment of time and, if it seem good to Him, recreate it in an instant. Nothing is difficult to Him, whether it be the creation of a fly or that of the seven heavens. He receives neither profit nor loss from whatever may happen. If all the infidels became believers and all the irreligious pious, He would gain no advantage. On the other hand, if all believers became infidels, He would suffer no loss.

He who repeats this Name will have long life.

AL-QAYYŪM

THE SELF-SUBSISTING

اَللّٰهُ لَاۤ اِلٰهَ اِلَّا هُوَ الْحَىُّ الْقَيُّوْمُ ط

Allāh! There is no god save Him, the Alive, the Self-Subsisting. (3 : 2)

Al-Qayyūm is an Attribute of Allāh which means the Self-Subsisting. He does not depend on anything. nor does He require any support. He is Omnipotent, Ominscient, Creator and Sustainer of all things.

He is Almighty and the sole Provider. He sustains the existence of everything and is Himself sustained or supported by no body. By the mere mention of Life and Self-Subsistence as His two essential attributes the possibility of all co-partnership with Him is negatived outright. Allāh is called *Al-Qayyūm* because He is the Self-Subsisting, Living Lord Who judgeth all.

He who repeats this Name will never fall into inadvertency.

AL-WĀHID
THE ONE

الْوَاحِد جَلَّ جَلَالُهُ

يَوْمَ هُمْ بَارِزُوْنَ لَا يَخْفَى عَلَى اللهِ مِنْهُمْ شَيْءٌ لِمَنِ الْمُلْكُ الْيَوْمَ لِلّٰهِ الْوَاحِدِ الْقَهَّارِ ٥

The day when they come forth, nothing of them being hidden from Allāh, Whose is the sovereignty this day? It is Allāh's, the One, the Almighty.
(40 : 16)

Al-Wāhid is the Name of Allāh because He is the Only One to be worshiped; the only One having neither beginning nor end; the only One Who is Eternal and shall remain for ever; the only One Who is Omnipotent, Omniscient. Omnipresent and nothing is hidden from Him, the only One Who is born to none and none is born to Him, and He has no partner or sharer. He is the only One to Whom all of us are answerable for our deeds. He is aware of every thought and act we think of or commit in every instant and breath of our life. He is the only One before Whom we have to render account of virtuous and sinful acts on the Day of Judgment, and accordingly decrees of rewards and penalties will be issued by Him only at His will and pleasure. Hence, He is the only One to be feared, obeyed, loved, adored and worshipped by one and all. Allāh is called *Al-Wāhid* because He is One in His actions and in His Names, He has no partner or equal in His Attributes, personality and orders.

He who repeats this Name alone and in a quiet place will be free from fear and delusion if God, the Most High, willeth.

AL-AHAD

THE ONE

Say : He is Allāh, the One. (112 : 1)

Al-Ahad is a name of Allāh synonymous to the other name *Wahid*, with slight difference and more emphasis on the Unity, hence it is more specific and reserved for Allāh only. The word *Wahid* besides denoting the name of Allāh, is normally used for other things as well, whereas it is not so in the case of *Ahad*. The name *Ahad* also stands even more specifically, for all the attributes signified by the other name *Wahid*. Hence, all these attributes mentioned previously for *wahid*, may be considered applicable to the word *Ahad*.

He who repeats this Name 1000 times, secrets of the universe will be opened to him. By reciting this sacred name of Allāh, one gets peace and contentment as well as Divine blessings.

AS-SAMAD
THE ETERNAL

Allāh, the eternally besought of all! (112 : 2)

As-Samad is a name of Allāh which conveys the sense that He is free from all wants and physical needs of living creatures necessary for performing their normal functions of life such as eating, drinking etc., and He is also free from all defects, weaknesses, liabilities and other attributes of worldly creatures. He knows, sees, hears and controls all things, events, thoughts and feelings that exist and happen outwardly or occur inwardly in the brains and hearts of all kinds of creatures. In other words He is Omnipersent, Omnipotent, Omniscient, All-Powerful, Complete and Perfect in every respect, and all His attributes are beyond description and imagination. He is not in need of anything, any service, any duty, any worship from any being or creature for Himself. It is the entire Universe and all the creatures living in it which need His Commands, awards and blessings. Hence we must worship Him with sincere feelings and firm belief, always fearing that we may not incur His displeasure by any of our acts and deeds and we must solicit His blessings and guidance on the right path. Allāh is the Only Being to apply to if one has any need to be fulfilled or any trouble to be eliminated.

He who repeats this Name frequently, Allāh will provide his needs, and as a result thereof he will not need others, but they will need him.

AL-QĀDIR

THE ABLE

قُلْ هُوَ الْقَادِرُ عَلَى اَنْ يَبْعَثَ عَلَيْكُمْ عَذَابًا مِنْ فَوْقِكُمْ اَوْ مِنْ تَحْتِ اَرْجُلِكُمْ اَوْ يَلْبِسَكُمْ شِيَعًا وَّ يُذِيْقَ بَعْضَكُمْ بَأْسَ بَعْضٍ ط

Say: He is Able to send punishment upon you from above you or from beneath your feet, or to bewilder you with dissension and make you taste the tyranny one of another. (6 : 65)

Al-Qādir is an Attribute of Allāh which manifests His power. He is Almighty. If He wills, He can raise the dead, make stones talk, trees walk, annihilate the Heavens and the Earth, and recreate of gold or of silver thousands similar to those destroyed. He can transport a man in a moment of time from the east to the west, or from the west to the east, or to the seventh heaven. His power is eternal a *priori* and a *posteriori*. It is not posterior to His essence.

He who recites this Name, all his desires will be fulfilled.

AL-MUQTADIR

THE POWERFUL

كَذَّبُوْا بِاٰيٰتِنَا كُلِّهَا فَاَخَذْنٰهُمْ اَخْذَ
عَزِيْزٍ مُّقْتَدِرٍ ۟

Who denied Our revelations, every one. There-fore, We grasped them with the grasp of the Mighty, the Powerful. (54 : 42)

Al-Muqtadir is an Attribute of Allāh which is synony-mous to His attribute *Qadir*. To form an idea of His attribute related to these two names *Qadir* and *Muqtadir*, we must ponder over the verses in which the names *Awwal, Akhir, Zahir* and *Batin* have been used.

"Allāh has power over everything": He gives life and also death: He causes the rise and the downfall. It is by His command that the seasons change. Therefore, if any community is enjoying prosperity today, it should be under no delusion that this condition will remain for ever. That God, by Whose command these things have been bestowed on it, has the power to snatch away all this by another command. Allāh is called *Al-Muqtadir* because He is more powerful than any being.

He who repeats this Name will be aware of the truth

AL-AWWAL
THE FIRST

هُوَالْاَوَّلُ وَالْاٰخِرُ وَالظَّاهِرُ وَالْبَاطِنُ ۚ وَهُوَبِكُلِّ شَىْءٍ عَلِيمٌ ٥

He is the First and the Last, and the Outward and the Inward; and He is Knower of all things.
(57 : 3)

Al-Awwal is a name of Allāh, that shows and establishes His Being prior to and before anything or any being existed *i.e.,* from Eternity. He is prior and superior to all things, creatures or beings, that have ever come into existence. The beginning of instructions, orders, commands, thoughts, intentions, sounds from far and near, act, happenings, events, intellect, knowledge, wisdom, besides all worldly, physical and spiritual matters are from Him and at His will.

He who would like to have a child but cannot, or would like to have nearness to a fellow-traveller, repeats this Name 1,000 times for 40 Fridays, his desires will be fulfilled if God, the Most High, willeth.

AL-ĀKHIR
THE LAST

آلْاَخِرُ جَلَّ جَلَالُهُ

هُوَالْاَوَّلُ وَالْاَخِرُ وَالظَّاهِرُ وَالْبَاطِنُ وَهُوَ بِكُلِّ شَىْءٍ عَلِيْمٌ ٥

*He is the First and the Last, and the Outward
and the Inward; and He is Knower of all things.*
(57 : 30)

Al-Ākhir is a name of Allāh, showing that He shall
remain for ever, even after everything is annihilated.
After the end of all creatures and beings, that must
necessarily happen to all things which have ever come into
existence, He shall remain for ever. All the conditions,
happenings and events which take place on the earth and
in the heavens will be ended. There will also be an end to
all thoughts, intentions, knowledge, intellect, wisdom,
sounds, sight, hearing etc. But He is Final and Perfect in
every respect. He is therefore, called *Ākhir*. This name is
always accompanied by the previous one, and both of
them appear as *Al-Awwal-wal-Ākhir*.

He who repeats this Name frequently will not only
lead a happy life in this world but will also have a happy
ending.

AZ-ZAHIR

THE MANIFEST

He is the First and the Last and the Evident and the Hidden; and He is Knower of all things.
(57 : 3)

Az-Zahir is one of the ninety-nine Attributes of Allāh, which means "the Manifest". Allāh is *az-Zahir* because His Signs are everywhere evident in the whole universe. Allāh is the Manifest and nothing is hidden from Him. There is nothing that men can do but Allāh is a witness to it. His knowledge not only comprehends all things, but has all things actively before it. Allāh's all embracing knowledge is independent of time, or place or circumstances.

He who recites this Name fifteen times after Friday (*Jum'a*) Prayer, divine light (*Nūr*) will enter his heart.

Recitation of this sacred name of Allāh five hundred times, after *Ishraq* prayer (an optional *salat* offered soon after sunrise) invigorates the eye-sight; and prayers made to Allāh are granted through His Mercy.

AL-BĀTIN

THE HIDDEN

هُوَالْاَوَّلُ وَالْاٰخِرُوَالظَّاهِرُ وَالْبَاطِنُ ج وَهُوَ بِكُلِّ شَىْءٍ عَلِيْمٌ ٥

*He is the First and the Last, and the Evident
and the Hidden; and He is Knower of all things.*
(57 : 3)

Al-Bātin is one of the ninety-nine special Names of
Allāh. It means "that which is hidden or concealed,"
"The Hidden One," or "He that knows hidden things"

Bātin means that which is within, as opposed to
that which is evident in things outside. Allāh has both
these qualities. His Signs are everywhere evident in the
whole universe. But He is also immanent within us and in
the soul of all good things. The pair of seemingly opposite
qualities, First and Last, Evident and Immanent, are
referred to here, to point the contrast with our human
frailty, in which monasticism may not be the same as
humility, spending may not be the same as charity, and
so on.

He who repeats this Name three times each day will
be able to see the truth in things.

AL-WĀLI
THE GOVERNOR

لَهُ مُعَقِّبَتٌ مِّنْ بَيْنِ يَدَيْهِ وَمِنْ خَلْفِهِ يَحْفَظُوْنَهُ مِنْ اَمْرِ اللّٰهِ ۗ اِنَّ اللّٰهَ لَا يُغَيِّرُ مَا بِقَوْمٍ حَتّٰى يُغَيِّرُوْا مَا بِاَنْفُسِهِمْ ۗ وَاِذَآ اَرَادَ اللّٰهُ بِقَوْمٍ سُوْٓءًا فَلَا مَرَدَّ لَهٗ ۚ وَمَا لَهُمْ مِّنْ دُوْنِهٖ مِنْ وَّالٍ ٥

For him are angels ranged before him and behind him, who guard him by Allāh's Command. Lo! Allāh changeth not the condition of a folk until they (first) change that which is in their hearts; and if Allāh willeth misfortune for a folk there is ·none that can repel it, nor have they any governor beside Him. (13 : 11)

Al-Wāli is an Attribute of Allāh which means "the Governor". It is Allāh only Who directs, manages, conducts, governs, measures, plans every action which happens at any moment in the entire universe. Allāh not only directly watches over whatever each person does, and is fully aware of everything he does, but He has also appointed such Guardians as accompany him everywhere and keep a full record of all his deeds. So those people have been warned who live their lives under the delusion that they have been left absolutely free to do whatever they like and shall not be required to render an account of what they did in this worldly life. These people invite their own retribution. When once the punishment comes, there is no turning it back. None of the things which he relied upon other than Allāh—can possibly protect him.

He who repeats this Name and breathes it into his house, his house will be free from danger.

AL-MUTA'ĀLI
THE MOST EXALTED

عَلِمُ الْغَيْبِ وَالشَّهَادَةِ الْكَبِيرُ الْمُتَعَالِ

*He is the Knower of the invisible and the visible,
the Great, the Most Exalted.* (13 : 9)

Al-Muta'āli is one of the ninety-nine Names or
Attributes of Allāh. He is called *Muta'āli* because He is
the Most Great, the Most Exalted, the Lofty One. He is
higher than any action, manner or condition, and any
thought that any being may have. This Name indicates
that Allāh is higher than the most evolved thought of
man.

He who repeats this Name frequently will gain the
benevolence of Allāh. Recitation of this sacred name of
Allāh restores the lost capabilities, power and prestige.

AL-BARR

THE SOURCE OF ALL GOODNESS

اِنَّا كُنَّا مِنْ قَبْلُ نَدْعُوهُ ط اِنَّهُ هُوَ الْبَرُّ الرَّحِيمُ ه

*Lo! we used to pray unto Him of old. Lo!
He is the Benign, the Merciful.* (52 : 28)

Al-Barr is one of the ninety-nine special Attributes
of Allāh. In its ordinary sense it means "pious" or "good".
As applied to Allāh, it means "The Beneficent One".
Allāh is tolerant to His servants, to all creatures, and is
good to them.

He who repeats this Name over his child, this child
will be free from misfortune. Parents who lose their children very young, should not despair for Allāh Almighty
in all His kindness and mercy shall bless them with children who shall survive if they recite profusely this sacred
name.

AT-TAWWĀB

جَلَّ جَلَالُه

THE ACCEPTER OF REPENTANCE

غَافِرِالـذَّنْبِ وَقَابِلِ التَّوْبِ شَـدِيدِ الْعِقَابِ ذِى الطَّوْلِ لَاۤ اِلٰهَ اِلَّا هُوَ اِلَيْهِ الْمَصِيرُ ٥

The Forgiver of sin, the Accepter of repentance, the Stern in punishment, the Bountiful. There is no god save Him. Unto Him is the journeying.
(40 : 3)

At-Tawwab is another *Attribute of Allāh*. The Messenger of Allāh (peace and blessings of Allāh be upon him), during his return journey from a military expedition or *Hajj* or *'Umrah*, used to recite *Allāh-u-Akbar* (Allāh is Supreme) thrice on every elevated ground that he came across and then recite the following supplication:

There is no deity save God. He is Alone. He hath no partner. Unto Him belongeth the sovereignty, and unto Him belongeth the praise. He is All-Powerful. We are turners (unto Allāh), penitents, worshippers, prostrators before our Lord, (and His) extollers. Allāh fulfilled His promise, helped His bondman, and alone routed the clans.

According to Islamic Shari'ah the validity of *Tauba* depends upon the following three things:

(a) Confession of One's sin.
(b) Remorse Contrition.
(c) A firm resolution to abstatin from its recurrence.

He who repeats this Name frequently, his repentance will be accepted.

AL-'AFUW

THE PARDONER

اِنْ تُبْدُوْا خَيْرًا اَوْ تُخْفُوْهُ اَوْ تَعْفُوْا عَنْ
سُوْٓءٍ فَاِنَّ اللّٰهَ كَانَ عَفُوًّا قَدِيْرًا ۞

If ye do good openly or keep it secret, or forgive evil, Lo! Allāh is Forgiving, Powerful. (4 : 149)

Al- Afuw is another Attribute of Allāh which means "One Who pardons or cancels", "The Pardoner (of sins)." Allāh pardons all who repent sincerely as if they had no previous sins. God forgives what is wrong and is Able fully to appreciate and judge of the value of our good deeds whether we publish them or conceal them.

He who repeats this Name frequently, Allāh will forgive all his sins. Those who recite this sacred name of Allāh and thereafter pray : "O' Allāh, Thou are the forgiver and likes to forgive, pray forgive my sins", Allāh Almighty will forgive his sins."

AR-RA'UF
THE COMPASSIONATE

الرَّءُوف جَلَّ جَلَالُهُ

وَلَوْلَافَضْلُ اللهِ عَلَيْكُمْ وَرَحْمَتُهُ
وَاَنَّ اللهَ رَءُوفٌ رَّحِيمٌ ۞

Were it not for the grace and mercy of Allāh on you, and that Allāh is full of kindness and mercy.
(24 : 20)

Ar-Ra'uf is one of the ninety-nine Attributes of Allāh which means "The Compassionate". Allāh is full of kindness and mercy. One should observe purity in act and in thought, concerning one's self and concerning others; it is only God's grace that can keep that purity spotless, for He hears all prayers and knows all the temptations to which, human nature is subject. His Will and Plan make both for spiritual protection and spiritual peace, and we must place ourselves trustingly in His hands.

He who repeats this Name frequently will be blessed by Allāh. The recitation of this sacred name of Allāh turns a harsh and hard master into a kind and lenient one.

AL-JĀME‘

THE GATHERER

رَبَّنَا اِنَّكَ جَامِعُ النَّاسِ لِيَوْمٍ لَّا رَيْبَ فِيهِ ط اِنَّ اللهَ لَا يُخْلِفُ الْمِيعَادَ ة

Our Lord! it is Thou Who gatherest mankind together to a Day of which there is no doubt. Lo! Allāh faileth not to keep the tryst. (3 : 9)

Al-Jāme‘ is an Attribute of Allāh which means "the Gatherer". Allāh is *al-Jāme* because he is One Who collects things, gathers them, anywhere He wants, at any time.

He who repeats this Name will find the things that he lost. One who has been separated from his people, family or friends, may recite this sacred name of Allāh, and He in all His kindness and mercy shall reunite them.

AL-GHANĪ
THE SELF-SUFFICIENT

يَا أَيُّهَا النَّاسُ أَنْتُمُ الْفُقَرَآءُ إِلَى اللهِ وَاللهُ هُوَ الْغَنِيُّ الْحَمِيدُ

O' mankind ye are the poor in your relation to Allāh. And Allāh! He is the Self-Sufficient, the Owner of Praise. (35 : 15)

Al-Ghani is one of the ninety-nine special Names or Attributes of Allāh, expressing the superiority of the Almighty over the necessities and requirements of mankind. If anyone rejects God's Message or Law, the loss is his own. It is not God Who needs him or his worship or his sacrifice or his praise. It is man that depends on God and has need of Him every moment of his life. God is independent of all wants, and His attributes are inherently deserving of all praise, whether the wicked give such praise or not, in word or deed.

Allāh is not dependent on our prayer or service. It is out of His Mercy that He desires our own good. Any race or people to whom He gives chances should understand that its failure does not affect God. He could create others in their place, as He did in times past, and is doing in our own day if only we had the wit to see it.

He who repeats this Name will be contented and covetous.

AN-NŪR

THE LIGHT

اَللّٰهُ نُوْرُ السَّمٰوٰتِ وَالْاَرْضِ ط

Allāh is the Light of the Heavens and the Earth.
(24 : 35)

An-Nūr is an Attribute of Allāh which means "The Light". God Most High is the only Reality, as He is the Only Light. That Ultimate Light is the final Fountainhead, Who is Light in and by Himself, not a light kindled from other lights. The physical light is but a reflection of the true Light in world of Reality, and the true Light is God. We can only think of God in terms of our phenomenal experience, and in the phenomenal world, light is the purest thing we know But physical light has drawbacks incidental to its nature e.g.,(1) it is dependent upon some source external to itself; (2) it is a passing phenomenon; if we take it to be a form of motion or energy it is unstable, like all physical phenomena; (3) it is dependent on space and time; its speed is 186,000 miles per second, and there are stars whose light takes thousands of years before it reaches the earth. The perfect Light of God is free from any such defects.

The Messneger of Allāh (peace and blessings of Allāh be upon him) says: "God has Seventy Thousand veils of Light. . . . " Jibra'īl says "Between me and Him are seventy thousand veils of Light".

As all our Lights have their source in the great Primary Light, the One Reality, there can be no light unless God gives the Light.

He who repeats this Name will have inner light.

AL-HĀDI
THE GUIDE

وَكَذَٰلِكَ جَعَلْنَا لِكُلِّ نَبِيٍّ عَدُوًّا مِّنَ الْمُجْرِمِينَ ۗ وَكَفَىٰ بِرَبِّكَ هَادِيًا وَنَصِيرًا ۝

Even so have We appointed unto every Prophet an opponent from among the guilty; but Allāh sufficeth for a Guide and Helper. (25 : 31)

Hadi is a Name of Allāh, signifying His attribute of guidance to the right path. This guidance is classified as follows:

(1) Guidance of Allāh meant for all creations, including minerals, plants, animals etc.

(2) Guidance from Allāh, which was preached by His Messengers to their followers.

(3) Guidance from Allāh, which may be defined as divine help.

(4) Divine guidance by which the righteous believers shall attain their salvation in the Hereafter.

Allāh is called *Hādi*, because He guides His righteous people through intuition and inspiration. He imparts wisdom to His faithful servants and guides them to the right path. However the sinners, liars, infidels and swindlers are debarred from His guidance.

He who recites this Name will have spiritual knowledge.

AL-BADI‘

THE ORGINATOR

بَدِيعُ السَّمٰوٰتِ وَالْاَرْضِ ط وَاِذَا قَضٰى اَمْرًا فَاِنَّمَا يَقُوْلُ لَهٗ كُنْ فَيَكُوْنُ ٥

The Originator of the heavens and the earth!
When He decreeth a thing, He saith unto it
only Be! and it is. (2 : 117)

Al-Badi' is one of the ninety-nine special Attributes of Allāh. It means "He Who originates". Allāh creates wonders in the universe without any design.

He who repeats this Name 70 times in the following way, all his troubles will disappear:

Ya Badee'i as-Semavati wal-ard: O' He Who is the Originator of incomparable things in the heavens and on the earth.

Recitation of this sacred name of Allāh is invaluable for the accomplishment of a difficult task or the attainment of a difficult objective.

RABB

THE SUSTAINER

اِنَّ اللّٰهَ رَبِّیْ وَرَبُّکُمْ فَاعْبُدُوْهُ ط هٰذَا صِرَاطٌ مُّسْتَقِیْمٌ ۰

Lo! Allāh is my Lord and your Lord, so worship Him. That is a straight path. (3 : 51)

The Arabic word *Rabb* is usually translated as Lord. The word "Lord" by itself is an inadequate rendering for *Rabb*. For it implies cherishing, guarding from harm, sustaining, granting all the means and opportunities of development. Allāh is the Lord of the universe in all these senses. Allāh cares for all the worlds He has created. For shortness, perhaps "Guardian Lord" will be sufficient.

By recitation of this sacred name of Allāh as many times as possible, ways and means will open up for the best possible up-bringing of the children. There shall also be safety against dangers of all kinds.

MUBIN

مُبِيْن جَلَّ جَلَالُهُ

THE MANIFEST

يَوْمَئِذٍ يُّوَفِّيْهِمُ اللّٰهُ دِيْنَهُمُ الْحَقَّ وَيَعْلَمُوْنَ اَنَّ اللّٰهَ هُوَ الْحَقُّ الْمُبِيْنُ ۝

On that day Allāh will pay them their just dues and they will know that Allāh, He is the Manifest Truth. (24 : 25)

Mubin implies both openness and clearness *i.e.*, freedom from ambiguity. As applied to Allāh, it means "The Manifest".

All that we thought of hiding will be clear as day before God's Judgment-Seat, because He is the very essence of Truth and Reality. He is the true Light of which all physical light is merely a type or reflection.

Our Faith tells us that Allāh is the Manifest Truth. Allah will deliver us from all harm if we sincerely repent and lead righteous lives. The unbelievers have no such hope. When the real adjustment of values is established, they will soon see whether we were in the wrong or they.

There is nothing that men can do but God is a witness to it. We may be deeply engrossed in some particular thing and for the time being be quite unconscious of other things. But God's knowledge not only comprehends all things. but has all things actively before it. Nothing is hidden from Him. And His knowledge has another quality which human knowledge has not. Human knowledge is subject to time, and is obliterated by time. God's knowledge is like a Record and endures for ever. And His Record has a further quality which human records have not. The most permanent human record may be quite intelligible to those who make it but may be ambiguous to others and may become unintelligible with the progress of time, as happens almost invariably to the most enduring inscription from very ancient times; but in God's "Record" or Knowledge there is no ambiguity, for it is independent of time, or place, or circumstance.

Allāh's all embracing knowledge and constant watchful care over all His creatures may be a source of fear to sinners, but there is no fear for those whom He honours with His love and friendship, neither in this world nor in the world to come.

AL-QADIR

THE MIGHTY

وَاللهُ خَلَقَكُمْ ثُمَّ يَتَوَفّٰىكُمْ قف وَمِنْكُمْ
مَّنْ يُّرَدُّ اِلٰٓى اَرْذَلِ الْعُمُرِ لِكَىْ لَا يَعْلَمَ
بَعْدَ عِلْمٍ شَيْئًا ط اِنَّ اللهَ عَلِيْمٌ قَدِيْرٌ ۰

*It is Allāh Who creates you and takes your
ouls at death; And of you there are some who
are sent back to a feeble age, so that they know
nothing after having known (much): For Allāh
is All-Knowing, All-Powerful.* (16 : 70)

Al-Qadir is one of the ninety-nine Attributes of
Allāh which means "the Mighty". Allāh not only provides
us with the necessities and good things of life but has full
power over our life and death. None else has any power
to give life or cause death. Besides the mystery and beauty of the many processes going on in the working of God's
creation, there is the wonderful life of man himself on
this earth: how he is created as a child; how he grows in
intelligence and knowledge; and how his soul is taken
back and his body suffers dissolution. In some cases he
lives so long that he falls into a feeble old age like a
second childhood; he forgets what he learnt and seems
almost to go back in Time. Is not all this wonderful, and
evidence of the Knowledge and Power of God.

While performing ablution if one keeps reciting this name of Allāh, it will bring him ascendancy over his foes and freedom from dangers.

AL-HĀFIZ

اَلْحَافِظُ جَلَّ جَلَالُهُ

THE PROTECTOR

فَاللهُ خَيْرٌ حِفْظًاص وَهُوَ اَرْحَمُ الرَّاحِمِينَ ٥

Allāh is better Protector, and He is the Most Merciful of those who show mercy. (12 : 64)

Al-Hāfiz is one of the ninety-nine Attributes of Allāh which means "the Protector". If man has a true spiritual understanding, he has nothing to be afraid of. He is protected by God in many ways that he does not even know. Allāh is also the Guardian of the Holy Qur'ān:

اِنَّا نَحْنُ نَزَّلْنَا الذِّكْرَ وَاِنَّا لَهُ لَحَافِظُونَ ٥

We have, without doubt, sent down the Message; and We will assuredly Guard it (from corruption). (15 : 9)

The Holy Qur'ān is the Word of Allāh and He is preserving it; therefore no one can do any harm to it; nor can discredit it by his ridicules, taunts and objections; nor can hamper its progress, whatever he may do against it; nor will anyone be ever able to change or tamper with it.

By oft-repeating and carrying this sacred name of Allāh on one's person, calamities are kept away.

AL-KAFIL

الكَفِيْل جَلَّ جَلَالُه

THE SURETY

وَأَوْفُوْا بِعَهْدِ اللهِ إِذَا عَاهَدْتُّمْ وَلَا
تَنْقُضُوا الْأَيْمَانَ بَعْدَ تَوْكِيدِهَا وَقَدْ
جَعَلْتُمُ اللهَ عَلَيْكُمْ كَفِيْلًا ط

*Fulfil your covenant with Allāh when you have
made a covenant with Him, and break not your
oaths after the asseveration of them, and after
ye have made Allāh surety over you.* (16 : 91)

Al-Kafil is one of the ninety-nine Attributes of Allāh
which means "The Surety". If one wants a real witness,
it is not these sorts of fancy miracles, but the witness of
the true Ever-living God. God is always every where –
and with us. We should purify our hearts, and ask Him in
true contrition and repentance, and He will guide us
and show us the Way. God knows all and He is the Real
Witness.

Recitation of this sacred name of Allāh twenty one
times every morning, inculcates good manners and good
morals in one's children.

ASH-SHĀKIR
THE APPRECIATIVE

And whosoever does good of his own accord, then Allāh is Appreciative (of his good deeds and) All-Knowledge. (2:158)

Shākir like *Shakūr* when applied to God means, "He Who approves, or rewards, or forgives, much, or largely: He Who gives large reward for small, or few works". Or, One Who highly appreciates good and is Bountiful in rewarding it.

There is no pleasure nor advantage to God in punishing His own creatures, over whom He watches with loving care. On the contrary He appreciates and recognises any good—however little—which He finds in us, and delights to give us a reward beyond all measures. His recognition of us is compared by a bold metaphor to our gratitude to Him for His favours. This epithet *Shākir* is applied to God

This auspicious name of Allāh has invaluable blessings for those whose means of livelihood are limited, or those who suffer from poor eye-sight. If such people recite this sacred name every day forty one times over a cup of water and rub it on their breast and eyes, there will be a change for the better and the eye-sight shall improve.

AL-AKRAM 

THE MOST BOUNTEOUS

اِقۡرَاۡ وَرَبُّكَ الۡاَكۡرَمُ ۙ

Read: And thy Lord is the Most Bounteous.
(96 : 3)

Al-Akram is one of the ninety-nine Attributes of Allāh which means "the Most Bounteous". Allāh is the Most Bounteous because He sustains all the creations. All is the Most Bounteous because He bestows His favours upon His servants.

It is the kindness of Allāh that He revealed the Holy Qur'an for the guidance of mankind. Allāh is the Most Bounteous because by His Grace man is made the most eminent of all creations.

Allāh has shown grace to the believers by sending unto them the Messenger of Allāh (peace and blessings of Allāh be upon him). He exalted the Messenger of Allāh (peace and blessings of Allāh be upon him) to high rank and conferred upon him the honour of being the Noblest of all men.

The Messenger of Allāh (peace and blessings of Allāh be upon him) used to supplicate between as-Safa' and al-Marwah the following prayer:

رَبِّ اغْفِرْ وَارْحَمْ اَنْتَ الْاَعَزُّ الْاَكْرَمُ

Lord of mine! Pardon, and have mercy!
Most Powerful, Most Bounteous art
Thou! (Hisn Hasin)

AL-A'LA

THE MOST HIGH

Praise the name of thy Lord the Most High.
(87 : 1)

Al-A'la is one of the ninety-nine Attributes of Allāh which means "the Most High". Allāh is called *Al-A'la* because He is the Real King and above all. His name is *Al-A'la* because He is Most High and Mighty.

When the verse (89:1) was revealed, the Messenger of Allāh (peace and blessings of Allāh be upon him) said: Recite ye the prayer " سُبْحَانَ رَبِّىَ الْأَعْلَى " "Glory be to my Lord the Exalted" thrice in your *Sujud*.

AL-KHALLĀQ

THE CREATOR

Lo! Thy Lord! He is the All-Wise Creator.
(15 · 86)

Al-Khallāq is one of the ninety-nine Attributes of Allāh. *Khallāq:* the emphatic form, as meaning the Creator, Who is perfect in His Skill and Knowledge, and whose creation answers perfectly to His design. Therefore, no one should think that anything has gone wrong in Allāh's creation. What may seem out of joint is merely the result of our shortsighted standards. It often happens that what appears to us to be evil or imperfect or unjust is a reflection of our own imperfect mind.

Continued recitation of this name of Allāh in the quiet hours of a night, ensure continuity of blessings till the Day of Reckoning equal to that of an angel's devoted supplications.

AL-MAULĀ

THE POTECTOR

الْمَوْلٰى جَلَّ جَلَالُهُ

وَاِنْ تَوَلَّوْا فَاعْلَمُوٓا اَنَّ اللهَ مَوْلٰىكُمْ نِعْمَ الْمَوْلٰى وَنِعْمَ النَّصِيْرُ ۝

And if they turn away, then know that Allāh is your Protector —a transcendent Protector, a transcendent Helper! (8 : 40)

Maula is a term used in Islamic law for a freed slave, but in the Holy Qur'ān it is used for "a Protector or Helper", *i.e.*, Allāh Almighty. The Holy Qur'ān says:

ذٰلِكَ بِاَنَّ اللهَ مَوْلَى الَّذِيْنَ اٰمَنُوْا وَ اَنَّ الْكٰفِرِيْنَ لَا مَوْلٰى لَهُمْ ۝

That is because Allāh is the Protector of those who believe, but those who reject Allāh have no protector. (47 : 11)

رَبَّنَا وَلَا تُحَمِّلْنَا مَا لَا طَاقَةَ لَنَا بِهٖ ۚ وَاعْفُ عَنَّا ۖ وَاغْفِرْ لَنَا ۖ وَ ارْحَمْنَا ۖ اَنْتَ مَوْلٰنَا فَانْصُرْنَا عَلَى

الْقَوْمِ الْكَٰفِرِينَ ۝ ع

Our Lord! lay not on us a burden greater than we have strength to bear. Blot out our sins, and grant us forgiveness. Have mercy on us. Thou art our Protector; Help us against those who stand against Faith. (2 : 286)

We should pray to Allāh for His help not in our own selfish ends, but in our resolve to uphold God's Truth against all Unbelief.

AN-NASIR

THE HELPER

وَاللهُ اَعْلَمُ بِاَعْدَآئِكُمْ ط وَكَفٰى بِاللهِ وَلِيًّا ۚ وَّكَفٰى بِاللهِ نَصِيْرًا ۟

And Allāh knows well your enemies. And Allāh suffices as a Protector, and Allāh suffices as a Helper. (4 : 45)

An-Nasir is one of the ninety-nine Attributes of Allāh which means "the Helper". Allāh is *Naṣir* and His help appears in the shape of guidance. However, the disbelievers, disobedient and the arrogant are deprived to His help. Allāh is the true Helper. His help gives satisfaction and contentment to the believers and they bear the difficulties of the world with great courage.

All prayer must be for God's aid and authority. However much we may plan, our success must depend on His aid. However nobler our motives, we have no right to imperil any lives unless there is authority in the Word of Allāh.

Anas (Allāh be pleased with him) reported that when the Messenger of Allāh (peace and blessings of Allāh be upon him) went forth to battle, he would say:

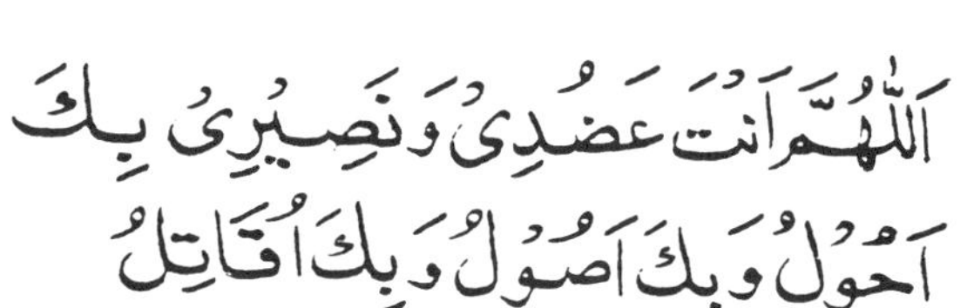

O' Allāh! Thou art mine arm and my helper. With Thy help do I move; with Thy help do I assail; and with Thy help do I battle. (Tirmidhi and *Abū Dāwūd)*

AL-ILĀH
GOD

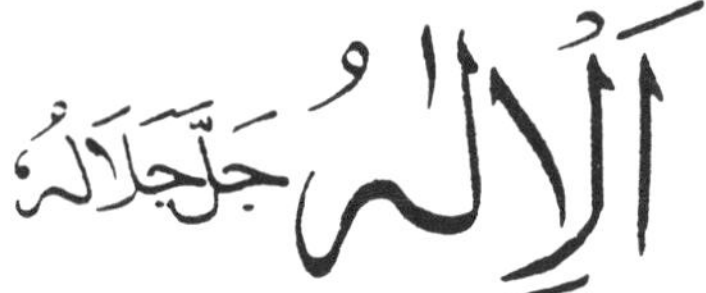

Say: What has come to me by inspiration is that your God is One Allāh. (21 : 108)

Al-Ilāh means God. God is One, and there is none other besides. The vulgar worship false gods out of fear that they would harm them or hope that they would confer some benefit on them. These false gods can do neither. All power, all goodness, is in the hands of the One True God. All else is pretence or illusion. There is but One God, the Universal Lord, Who made and loves and cherishes all.

AL-ALLĀM

THE OMNISCIENT

In the day when Allāh gathereth together the messengers, and saith: What was your response (from mankind)? They say: We have no knowledge. Lo! Thou, only Thou art the Knower of Things Hidden. (5 : 109)

Al-'Allām is one of the ninety-nine Attributes of Allāh which means "the Omniscient". Allāh is Al-'Allām because He knows all things and nothing is hidden from Him.

The Messenger of Allāh (peace and blessings of Allāh be upon him) said, when any one of you intendeth (doing) aught, let him offer two *rak'ahs* beside the obligatory prayer, then let him say:

O' Allāh! Behold, I ask of Thee the good through Thy knowledge, and ability through Thy power, and beg (Thy favours), out of Thine infinite bounty. For, behold Thou hast power; I have none. Thou knowest, I know not; and Thou art the Great Knower of things hidden. (Bukhāri)

AL-QĀHIR

THE OMNIPOTENT

He is the Omnipotent over His slaves, and He is the Wise, the Knower. (6 : 18)

Al-Qāhir is one of the ninety - nine Attributes of Allāh which means "the Omnipotent". Allāh is *Qāhir* because He holds complete dominance over all creations. Allāh is *Qāhir* because no body is equal to Him in Excellence and Attributes. Allāh is *Qāhir* because He has greater Commading influence over all creations. Abū Mas'ūd al-Anṣāri reported: I was assaulting my slave when I heard a voice behind me: Know, O' Abū Mas ud! Allāh is powerful over you more than what you have got over him. Then I looked when lo! he was the Messenger of Allāh (peace and blessings of Allāh be upon him). I said: O' Messenger of Allāh! he is free for the sake of Allāh. He said: Beware! Had you not done it, the Fire would surely have burnt you, or the Fire would have touched you. (*Muslim*)

The continued recitation of this name gives protection against the temptation of this world.

AL-GHĀFIR

THE FORGIVER

غَافِرِ الذَّنْبِ وَقَابِلِ التَّوْبِ شَدِيدِ الْعِقَابِ ذِى الطَّوْلِ لَآ اِلٰهَ اِلَّا هُوَ اِلَيْهِ الْمَصِيْرُ ۟

The Forgiver of sin, the Accepter of repentance, the Stern in punishment, the Bountiful. There is no god save Him. Unto Him is the journeying. (40 : 3)

Al-Ghāfir is one of the ninety-nine Attributes of Allāh which means "the Forgiver". God's knowledge is supreme and all-reaching. But there are other attributes of His, which concern us even more intimately *e.g.,* He forgives sin and accepts our repentance when it is sincere and results in our change of heart and life: but He is also just, and strict in punishment; and so no loophole will be left for Evil except in repentance. And further, all His attributes reach forward to everything: His Mercy, as well as His Knowledge and Justice; His Bounties as well as His Punishments. God's knowledge and attributes are perfect, and everything around us proclaims this. We are surrounded by His Signs. It is only want of Faith that will make people dispute about them.

AL-FĀTIR

THE CREATOR

الْحَمْدُ لِلّٰهِ فَاطِرِ السَّمٰوٰتِ وَالْأَرْضِ

Praise be to Allāh, Who created (out of nothing) the heavens and the earth. (35 : 1)

Al-Fātir is one of the ninety-nine Attributes of Allāh which means "the Creator". Allāh is *Fātir* because He has created the heavens and the earth. Allāh is *Fātir* because He is the Creator of nature and the natural law. Allāh is *Fātir* because nothing has gone wrong in His creation as He is perfect in His skill of creation. The word *Fātir* implies the creation of primeval matter, to which further creative processes have to be added by the hand of Allāh, for Allāh "adds to His Creations as He pleases", not only in quantity, but in qualities, functions, relations, and variations in infinite ways. Allāh's creation did not stop at some past time: it continues for He has all power, and His mercies are ever poured forth without stint.

AL-MALIK

THE SOVEREIGN

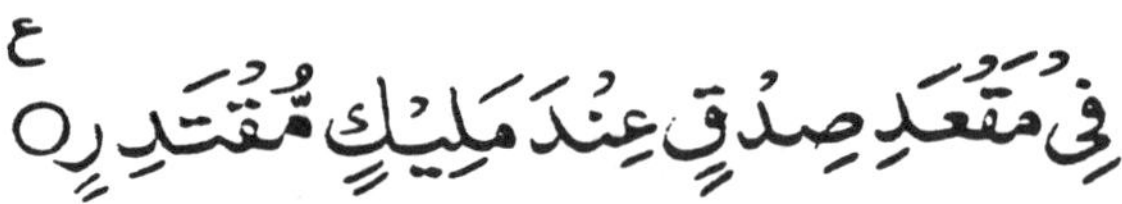

In an Assembly of Truth, in the Presence of a Sovereign Omnipotent. (54 : 55)

Al-Malik is one of the ninety-nine Attributes of Allāh which means "the Sovereign". God is Sovereign, All-in-all, First and Last, not only for ourselves but for all persons and things and events. God is present every-where and at all times.

The recitation of this sacred name softens the strains and enhances one's resources.

AL-HAFIYY

THE MOST GRACIOUS

قَالَ سَلَامٌ عَلَيْكَ سَاَسْتَغْفِرُ لَكَ رَبِّي اِنَّهُ كَانَ بِي حَفِيًّا

He said: Peace be unto thee! I shall ask forgive-
ness of my Lord for thee. Lo! He was ever
gracious unto me. (19 : 47)

The word *Ḥafiyy* signifies "well-disposed to, favour-
able to, good to, kind to". As applied to Allāh, it means
"The Most Gracious". Allāh is gracious to His servants, to
all creatures, and is good to them.

AL-MUHIT
ALL-PERVADING

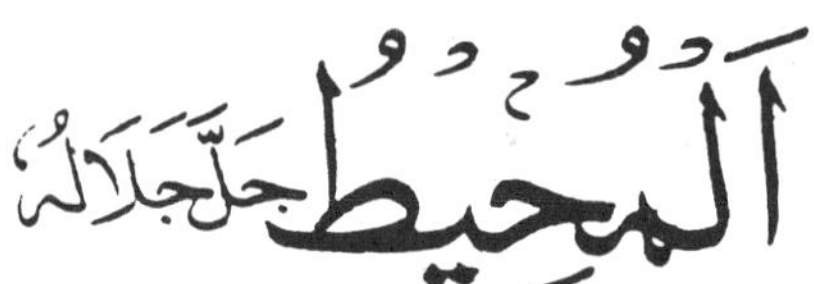

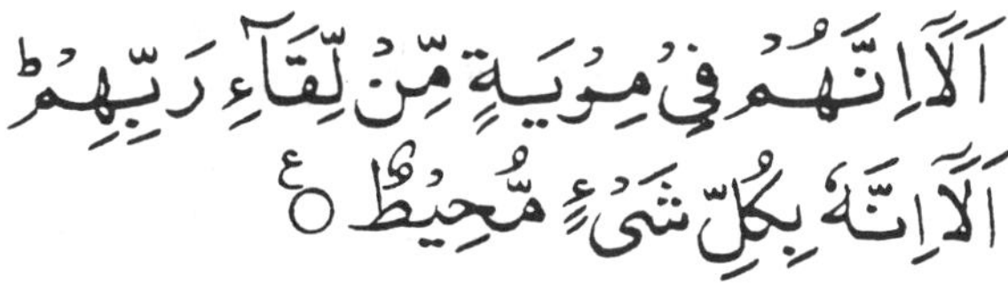

Ah indeed! Are they still in doubt about .e meeting with their Lord? Ah indeed! it is He that doth encompass all things. (41 : 54)

Al-Muhit is one of the ninety-nine Attributes of Allāh which means "the All-Pervading". Short-sighted people may like to think that there may be no Judgment. But Judgment is inevitable and cannot be escaped, for Allāh "doth encompass all things". Allāh, Most High, encompasses all things and is in the company of and is close to everything that exists by an encompassing, accompanying, and closeness of His own; not the sort that we can comprehend in our limited minds, as that is not worthy of His Sacred Being. Thus, it is our belief that the Almighty encompasses all things and that He is indeed close by, even though we do not comprehend the full significance of these terms.

Many a well-meaning persons feel some difficulty when it comes to offering their daily prayers (*Salāt*). Such persons should go to sleep with their hands on their bosom after reciting this sacred names seven times. They shall find their will and determination strengthened.

AL-MUSTA'ĀN

الْمُسْتَعَانُ جَلَّ جَلَالُهُ

ONE WHO IS CALLED UPON FOR HELP : GOD

قُلْ رَبِّ احْكُمْ بِالْحَقِّ ۚ وَرَبُّنَا الرَّحْمٰنُ الْمُسْتَعَانُ عَلٰى مَا تَصِفُوْنَ ۚ

He saith: My Lord! Judge Thou with truth, Our Lord is the Beneficent, Whose help is to be implored against that which ye ascribe (unto Him). (21 : 112)

Al-Musta'ān is one of the ninety-nine Attributes of Allāh meaning the One Who is called upon for help. We pray to Allāh for help because we know that He is the Lord of the whole Universe and He has powers and He is the Master of every thing. Therefore we turn to Allāh for help for the fulfilment of our needs and requirements. We worship Allāh alone and ask for His aid only. For there is none other than Allāh worthy of our devotion and able to help us.

It is reported in a tradition that the Messenger of Allāh (peace and blessings of Allāh be upon him) said to Mu'ādh bin Jabal: O' Mu'ādh! I love you. You should not forget to supplicate the following supplication after every Prayer:

O' Allāh to Thee is the praise, and to Thee I

complain, and to Thee I call for help, and Thou art the Helper. There is no strength or power except with Allāh.

AR-RAFI'

THE SUBLIME

*The Exalter of Ranks, the Lord of the Throne:
He casteth the Spirit of His command upon
whom He will of His slaves, that He may warn
of the Day of Meeting. (40 : 15)*

Al-Rafi' is one of the ninety-nine Attributes of
Allāh, which means "the Sublime". He is raised far above
any rank or degree which we can imagine. It is possible
also to treat *Rafi'* as equivalent to *Rafi'*, meaning that He
can raise His creatures to the highest ranks and degrees in
His spiritual kingdom, for He is the fountain of all honour.

He who repeats this Name 100 times day and night,
Allāh will make him higher as far as honour, richness and
merit are concerned.

AL-KĀFI
THE SUFFICIENT ONE

اَلَيۡسَ اللّٰهُ بِكَافٍ عَبۡدَهٗ ط وَيُخَوِّفُوۡنَكَ
بِالَّذِيۡنَ مِنۡ دُوۡنِهٖ ط وَمَنۡ يُّضۡلِلِ اللّٰهُ فَمَا
لَهٗ مِنۡ هَادٍ ○

Is not Allāh Sufficient for His servant? Yet they would frighten thee with those beside Him. He whom Allāh sendeth astray, for him there is no guide. (39 : 36)

Al-Kāfi is one of the ninety-nine Attributes of Allāh, which means "the Sufficient One." The righteous man will find Allāh enough for all the protection he needs, all the rest and peace he craves for, and all the happiness he can imagine. If the evil ones wish to frighten him with false gods, he knows that that is mere superstition. In the case of idols to whom worship is paid, this is easily intelligible. But there are other false gods which men worship, — wealth, position, power, science, selfish desire, and so on. The idea may occur to them: "this is the right course, but what will men say?" or "shall I lose my case if I tell the truth?" or "will it ruin my chances if I denounce sin in high places?" All such false gods will only mislead and leave their victims in the lurch. The worship of them will lose them the grace of Allāh, which wants to guide and comfort all who seek God. On the other hand if anyone holds fast to God's Truth, nothing can mislead or betray him.

wants to guide and comfort all who seek God. On the other hand if anyone holds fast to God's Truth, nothing can mislead or betray him.

GHĀLIB
THE PREDOMINANT

غَالِبُ جَلَّ جَلَالُهُ

وَاللّٰهُ غَالِبٌ عَلٰى اَمْرِهٖ وَلٰكِنَّ اَكْثَرَ النَّاسِ لَا يَعْلَمُوْنَ ۞

And Allāh was predominant in his career, but most of mankind know not. (12: 21)

Ghālib is an Attribute of Allāh which means "the Predominant". Allāh is full of might and majesty and is Able to enforce His Will.

AL-MANNĀN
THE MOST GRACIOUS

لَقَدْ مَنَّ اللّٰهُ عَلَى الْمُؤْمِنِينَ اِذْ بَعَثَ فِيهِمْ رَسُوْلًا مِّنْ اَنْفُسِهِمْ يَتْلُوْا عَلَيْهِمْ اٰيٰتِهٖ وَيُزَكِّيْهِمْ وَيُعَلِّمُهُمُ الْكِتٰبَ وَالْحِكْمَةَ ۚ وَاِنْ كَانُوْا مِنْ قَبْلُ لَفِىْ ضَلٰلٍ مُّبِيْنٍ ٥

Allāh verily hath shown grace to the believers by sending unto them a messenger of their own who reciteth unto them His revelations, and causeth them to grow, and teacheth them the Scripture and wisdom, although before (he came to them) they were in flagrant error. (3 : 164)

Al-Mannān is an Attribute of Allāh which means "the Most Gracious". The word *Mannān* is derived from the root *Mann* which means "gracious" or *minnat* meaning 'favour'. Allāh is *Al-Mannān* because He shows favour to His creations and bestows benefits on them.

Anas (Allāh be pleased with him) reported: Whilst I was sitting with the Messenger of Allah (peace and blessings of Allāh be upon him) in the mosque, a man was offering *Salāt*. (In the course of his prayer) the man said:

اَللّٰهُمَّ اِنِّىْ اَسْئَلُكَ بِاَنَّ لَكَ الْحَمْدَ لَاۤ اِلٰهَ اِلَّاۤ اَنْتَ الْحَنَّانُ الْمَنَّانُ بَدِيْعُ السَّمٰوٰتِ وَالْاَرْضِ يَا ذَا الْجَلَالِ وَالْاِكْرَامِ يَا حَيُّ يَا قَيُّوْمُ اَسْئَلُكَ

O' Allāh! Behold, I beg of Thee because unto Thee belongeth all praise. There is no god save Thee, the Most Relenting, the Most Gracious, the Originator of the heavens and the earth. O' Lord of Majesty and Glory, O' Living, Eternal One, of Thee I beg!

whereupon the Messenger of Allāh (peace and blessings of Allāh be upon him) said: (This man) called upon Allāh by His sublimest name. When He is called upon by that name He respondeth, and when He is besought in that name He bestoweth. (*Tirmidhi, Abū Dāwūd, Nasā'i* and *Ibn Majah*).

AL-JALIL
THE GLORIOUS

الْجَلِيْل جَلَّ جَلَالَه

تَبَارَكَ اسْمُ رَبِّكَ ذِى الْجَلَالِ وَ الْإِكْرَامِ ۚ

Blessed be the name of thy Lord, Mighty and Glorious! (55 : 78)

Al-Jalil, "the Glorious One", is an Attribute of Allāh. *Al-Jalal* is a term used by Sufi mystics to express that state of the Almighty which places Him beyond the understanding of His creatures.

The Messenger of Allāh (peace and blessings of Allāh be upon him) would on completing his *Salāt* turn round and say, thrice اَسْتَغْفِرُاللّٰه (I seek the forgiveness of Allah), then he would supplicate thus:

اَللّٰهُمَّ اَنْتَ السَّلَامُ وَمِنْكَ السَّلَامُ تَبَارَكْتَ يَا ذَا الْجَلَالِ وَالْإِكْرَامِ

O Allāh! Thou art the Peace and from Thee is Peace. Blessed art Thou, O' Lord of Majesty and Glory.

To recite this sacred name of Allāh, or to carry it on one's person, is a great blessing for enhancing one's prestige among his people.

AL-MUHYI
THE GIVER OF LIFE

Look, therefor, at the prints of Allāh's mercy (in creation): how He quickeneth the earth after death. Lo! He verily is the Quickener of the Dead, and He is Able to do all things. (30 : 59)

Al-Muhyi is one of the ninety-nine Attributes of Allāh which means "the Giver of Life". Allāh brings the dead to life. Even a little thinking on the right lines will convince every sensible and honest man that this process of bringing the dead to life is continuously going on before our eyes. Every human being has been created from a "dead" sperm drop. Then he gets life from "dead things" like food containing dead matter like coal, iron, lime, salts, gases which help make him a living human being. Then let us consider our surroundings. Seeds of different things which had been scattered here and there by the wind and birds and the root of different kinds of vegetation which lay rotten and dead in the soil, spring up to life as soon as there occurs a sprinkling of rain water. This process of the dead coming to life is observed during every rainy season year after year. The earth that dies in winter or drought lives again in spring or rain

by Allāh's Grace; so in the spiritual sphere, man may be dead and may live again by the Breath of Allāh and His Mercy if he will only place himself in Allāh's hands.

The baser self will come under control if this sacred name is recited on one's hands and then passed all over one's body.

AL-MUMIT 

THE GIVER OF DEATH

There is no god but He: it is He that giveth both life and death. (7 : 158)

Al-Mumit is one of the ninety-nine Attributes of Allāh which means "the Giver of death". The mysteries of life and death are in the hands of Allāh Who gives death to every living creature. When you die on this earth that is not the end. You were of Him, and you must return to Him. Allāh is All-Powerful and therefore can bring about Resurrection at any moment He wills. He can also bring back to life all the dead people just as He brought to life human beings out of nothing in the first instance. Allāh will hold the Last Judgment so that every one should get his due reward and his due punishment.

The baser self is subdued by frequently repeating this sacred name of Allāh. It opens a way for redemption from trials in the Herearter.

AL-WĀRITH
THE INHERITOR

And Verily, it is We Who give life and Who give death: it is We Who remain Inheritors (after all else passes away). (15 : 23)

Al-Wārith is one of the ninety-nine Attributes of Allāh which means "the Inheritor". To Allāh belongs the heritage of the heavens and the earth. Material wealth or property is only called ours during our short life, it then descends to heirs and heirs until it goes to the ultimate heir, the State. So all gifts are ours in trust only, they ultimately revert to Allāh, to Whom belongs all that is in the heavens or on earth. Allāh is called *al-Wārith* because all things proceed from Him and shall return into His hand.

One who recites this sacred name of Allāh becomes immune from the hardships and worries of this world and those of the Hereafter.

AL-BĀ'ITH

THE AWAKENER

وَاَنَّ السَّاعَةَ اٰتِيَةٌ لَّا رَيْبَ فِيهَا وَاَنَّ اللهَ يَبْعَثُ مَنْ فِى الْقُبُورِه

And because the Hour will come, there is no doubt thereof; and because Allāh will raise those who are in the graves. (22 : 7)

Al-Bā'ith is one of the ninety-names Attributes of Allāh. It means "He who awakes"; "The Awakener" (in the Day of Resurrection).

Allāh is *Al-Ba'ith* because He sent Messengers with glad tidings and warnings.

Allah is *Al-Bā'ith* because it is He Who has sent amongst the unlettered an Apostle from among themselves, to rehearse to them His Signs.

Allāh is *Al-Ba'ith* because ye shall indeed be raised up by Allah after your death.

Allāh is *Al-Bā'ith* because Allāh will raise up all who are in the graves.

Allāh is *Al-Bā'ith* because thy Lord will soon raise

thee (Prophet) to a station of Praise and Glory. He will assign the Messenger of Allāh (peace and blessings of Allāh be upon him) in the Hereafter the highest Post of Honour and Glory. *(the Maqām Mahmūd)*

With hands on one's bosom recitation of this sacred name of Allāh one hundred times every night before going to sleep shall bring Divine enlightenment to one's heart.

AL - BAQI
THE EVERLASTING

اَلْبَاقِی جَلَّ جَلَالُهُ

وَيَبْقَى وَجْهُ رَبِّكَ ذُو الْجَـلَالِ وَ
الْإِكْرَامِ

*There remaindeth but the Countenance
(Presence) of thy Rabb (Guardian Lord),
Majestic and Munificent.*

As we contemplate Allah's nature, we can use the most beautiful names we can think of, to express His attributes. There are hundreds of such attributes. For *tasbih* purposes a list of ninety nine names of Allah is made out in Hadith literature. As such *Al-Baqi* is the ninety ninth special name of Allah. It means "He Who remains"; The Everlasting One. Praise be to Allah Who was before Begining and will remain after the Ending. From His mercy came man's breath and unto Him returns the same.

The most magnificent works of man — such as they are — are but fleeting, Ships, Empires, the Wonders of Science and Art, the splendours of human glory or intellect, will all pass away. The most magnificent objects in outer Nature — the mountains and valleys, the sun and moon, the Constellation Orion and the star Sirins — will also pass away in their appointed time. But the only One that will endure for ever is the self (Presence) of Almighty Allah.

One who recites this sacred name of Allah is blessed with Divine knowledge and he who repeats this name 100 times before dawn will be free from all disasters throught his life and will be shown mercy in the Hereafter.

اَسْمَاءُ اللهِ الْحُسْنَى جَلَّ جَلَالُهُ وَعَمَّ نَوَالُهُ

NAMES AND ATTRIBUTES OF ALLĀH

Name or Attribute of Allāh	Transcription	Translation	Relevant Surah: Verse No.
اَللهُ	*Allāh*	God	*Ta Ha* : 14
اَلرَّحْمٰنُ	*Ar-Rahman*	The Compassionate	*Al-Baqarah*: 163
اَلرَّحِيْمُ	*Ar-Rahim*	The Merciful	*Fatihah* : 1-2
اَلْمَلِكُ	*Al-Mālik*	The Sovereign	*Ta Ha* : 114
اَلْقُدُّوْسُ	*Al-Quddūs*	The Holy	*Hashr* : 23
اَلسَّلَامُ	*As-Salām*	The Author of Safety	*Hashr* : 23
اَلْمُؤْمِنُ	*Al-Mu'min*	The Giver of Peace	*Hashr* : 23
اَلْمُهَيْمِنُ	*Al-Muhaimin*	The Protector	*Hashr* : 23
اَلْعَزِيْزُ	*Al-ʿAziz*	The Mighty One	*Hashr* : 23
اَلْجَبَّارُ	*Al-Jabbār*	The Compeller	*Hashr* : 23
اَلْمُتَكَبِّرُ	*Al-Mutakabbir*	The Majestic	*Hashr* : 23
اَلْخَالِقُ	*Al-Khāliq*	The Creator	*Hashr* : 24
اَلْبَارِئُ	*Al-Bāri'*	The Maker	*Hashr* : 24
اَلْمُصَوِّرُ	*Al-Mūsawwir*	The Fashioner	*Hashr* : 24
اَلْغَفَّارُ	*Al-Ghaffār*	The Great Forgiver	*Nūh* : 10

اَلْقَهَّارُ	*Al-Qahhār*	The Dominant	*Ra'd* : 16
اَلْوَهَّابُ	*Al-Wahhāb*	The Bestower	*Al-i-'Imran* : 18
اَلرَّزَّاقُ	*Ar-Razzāq*	The Provider	*Zariyat* : 58
اَلْفَتَاحُ	*Al-Fattāh*	The Judge	*Al-Sabā'* : 26
اَلْعَلِيمُ	*Al-'Alim*	The All-Knowing	*Al-Baqarah* : 115
اَلسَّمِيعُ	*As-Sami'*	The All-Hearing	*Al-i-'Imran* : 38
اَلْبَصِيرُ	*Al-Basir*	The All-Seeing One	*Al-i-'Imran* : 15
اَللَّطِيفُ	*Al-Latif*	The Subtle One	*Al-An'am* : 104
اَلْخَبِيرُ	*Al-Khabir*	The Aware	*Al-Saba'* : 1
اَلْحَلِيمُ	*Al-Halim*	The Clement	*Banu Isra'il* : 44
اَلْعَظِيمُ	*Al-'Azim*	The Great One	*Al-Baqarah* : 255
اَلْغَفُورُ	*Al-Ghafūr*	The All-Forgiving	*Mala'ikah* : 28
اَلشَّكُورُ	*Ash-Shakūr*	The Appreciative	*Mala'ikah* : 34
اَلْعَلِىُّ	*Al-'Aliyy*	The Sublime	*Shūrā* : 12
اَلْكَبِيرُ	*Al-Kabir*	The Most Great	*Saba'* : 23
اَلْحَفِيظُ	*Al-Hafiz*	The Preserver	*Hūd* : 57
اَلْمُقِيتُ	*Al-Mūqit*	The Maintainer	*Nisā'* : 85
اَلْحَسِيبُ	*Al-Hasib*	The Reckoner	*Nisā'* : 6
اَلْكَرِيمُ	*Al-Karim*	The Generous One	*Infitar* : 6
اَلرَّقِيبُ	*Al-Raqib*	The Watchful	*Nisā'* : 7
اَلْقَرِيبُ	*Al-Qarib*	The Nigh	*Hūd* : 61
اَلْمُجِيبُ	*Al-Mūjib*	The Responsive	*Hūd* : 61

اَلْوَاسِعْ	Al-Wāsi‘	The All-Embracing	Al-Baqarah 247
اَلْحَكِيمُ	Al-Hakim	The Wise	Al-Baqarah 129
اَلْوَدُودُ	Al-Wadūd	The Loving	Hūd : 90
اَلْمَجِيدُ	Al-Majid	The Most Glorious One	Hūd : 73
اَلشَّهِيدُ	Ash-Shahid	The Witness	Nisā’ : 79
اَلْحَقُّ	Al-Haqq	The Truth	Hajj : 6
اَلْوَكِيلُ	Al-Wakil	The Trustee	Nisā’ : 81
اَلْقَوِىُّ	Al-Qawi	The Most Strong	Hajj : 74
اَلْمَتِينْ	Al-Matin	The Firm One	Zariyat : 58
اَلْوَلِىُّ	Al-Wali	The Protecting Friend	Al-Baqarah : 257
اَلْحَمِيدُ	Al-Hamid	The Praiseworthy	Hajj : 64
اَلْحَىُّ	Al-Hayy	The Alive	Al-i-‘Imran : 2
اَلْقَيُّومُ	Al-Qayyūm	The Self-Subsisting	Al-i-‘Imran : 2
اَلْوَاحِدُ	Al-Wahid	The One	Mu’min : 16
اَلْاَحَدُ	Al-Ahad	The One	Ikhlas : 1
اَلصَّمَدُ	As-Samad	The Eternal	Ikhlas : 2
اَلْقَادِرُ	Al-Qādir	The Able	An‘ām : 65
اَلْمُقْتَدِرْ	Al-Muqtadir	The Powerful	Qamar : 42
اَلْاَوَّلْ	Al-Awwal	The First	Hadid : 3
اَلْاَخِرُ	Al-Ākhir	The Last	Hadid : 3

اَلظَّاهِرُ	Az-Zāhir	The Manifest	Hadid : 3
اَلْبَاطِنُ	Al-Bātin	The Hidden	Hadid : 3
اَلْوَالِى	Al-Wāli	The Governor	Ra'd : 11
اَلْمُتَعَالِى	Al-Muta'āli	The Most Exalted	Ra'd : 9
اَلْبَرُّ	Al-Barr	The Source of All Goodness	Tur : 28
اَلتَّوَّابُ	At-Tawwāb	The Accepter of Repentance	Mu'min : 3
اَلْعَفُوُّ	Al-'Afuw	The Pardoner	Nisā' : 149
اَلرَّءُوفُ	Ar-Ra'ūf	The Compassionate	Nūr : 20
اَلْجَامِعُ	Al-Jame'	The Gatherer	Al-i-'Imran : 9
اَلْغَنِىُّ	Al-Ghani	The Self-Sufficient	Mala'ikah : 15
اَلنُّوْرُ	An-Nūr	The Light	Nūr : 35
اَلْهَادِى	Al-Hadi	The Guide	Furqan : 31
اَلْبَدِيعُ	Al-Badi'	The Originator	Al-Baqarah : 117
اَلرَّبُّ	Rabb	The Sustainer	Al-i-'Imran : 51
اَلْمُبِيْنُ	Mubin	The Manifest	Nur : 25
اَلْقَدِيْرُ	Al-Qadir	The Mighty	Nahl : 70
اَلْحَافِظُ	Al-Hāfiz	The Protector	Yūsuf : 64
اَلْكَفِيْلُ	Al-Kafil	The Surety	Nahl : 91
اَلشَّاكِرُ	Ash-Shākir	The Appreciative	Al-Baqarah : 158
اَلْأَكْرَمُ	Al-Akram	The Most Bounteous	'Alq : 3
اَلْأَعْلَى	Al-A'la	The Most High	A'la : 7

اَلْخَلَّاقُ	Al-Khallāq	The Creator	Hijr : 86
اَلْمَوْلَى	Al-Maulā	The Patron	Anfal : 40
اَلنَّصِيرُ	An-Nasir	The Helper	Nisā' : 45
اَلْإِلَهُ	Al-ilāh	God	Ambiyā' : 108
اَلْعَلَّامُ	Al-'Allām	The Omniscient	Ma'ida : 112
اَلْقَاهِرُ	Al-Qāhir	The Omnipotent	An'am : 18
اَلْغَافِرُ	Al-Ghāfir	The Forgiver	Mu'min : 3
اَلْفَاطِرُ	Al-Fātir	The Creator	Shura : 11
اَلْمَلِيكُ	Al-Malik	The Sovereign	Qamar : 55
اَلْحَفِيُّ	Al-Hafiyy	The Gracious	Maryam : 47
اَلْمُحِيطُ	Al-Muhit	All-Pervading	Fussilat : 54
اَلْمُسْتَعَانُ	Al-Musta'ān	One Who is called upon for help: God	Ambiyā' : 112
اَلرَّفِيعُ	Al-Rafi'	The Sublime	Mu'min : 15
اَلْكَافِى	Al-Kāfi	The Sufficient One	Zumar : 36
غَالِبٌ	Ghālib	The Predominant	Yusuf : 21
اَلْمَنَّانُ	Al-Mannān	The Gracious	Al-i-'Imrān : 164
اَلْجَلِيلُ	Al-Jalil	The Glorious	Rahman : 78
اَلْمُحْى	Al-Muhyi	The Giver of Life	Rum : 50
اَلْمُمِيتُ	Al-Mumit	The Giver of Death	A'raf : 28
اَلْوَارِثُ	Al-Wārith	The Inheritor	Hijr : 23
اَلْبَاعِثُ	Al-Bā'ith	The Awakener	Hajj : 7
اَلْبَاقِى	Al-Bāqi	The Everlasting One	Rahman : 27

NAMES RELATING TO HIS KNOWLEDGE

Al-'Alim	The All-Knowing
Al-Hakim	The Wise
Al-Khabir	The Aware
Al-Sami'	The All-Hearing
Al-Basir	The All-Seeing One
Ash-Shahid	The Witness
Al-Raqib	The Watchful
Al-Bātin	The Hidden
Al-Qarib	The Nigh
Al-Kafil	The Surety
Al-'Allām	The Omniscient

NAMES RELATING TO HIS POWER AND CONTROL

Al-Qadir	The Mighty
Al-Wakil	The Trustee
Al-Hafiz	The Preserver
Al-Mālik	The Sovereign
Al-Fattāh	The Judge
Al-Hasib	The Reckoner
Al-Mūqit	The Maintainer
Al-Mūjib	The Responsive
Al-Bā'ith	The Awakener
Al-Mūhi	The Giver of Life
Al-Mūmit	The Giver of Death
Al-Jāme'	The Gatherer
Al-Bāqi	The Everlasting One
Al—Wārith	The Inheritor
Al-Hādi	The Guide
Al-Latif	The Subtle One
Al-Muqtadir	The Powerful
Al-Mūta'āli	The Most Exalted
Al-Mālik	The Sovereign
Al-Qadir	The Mighty
Al-Hafiz	The Protector
Al-Maulā	The Patron
Al-Qāhir	The Omnipotent
Al-Muhit	All-Pervading
Al-Muhaimin	The Protector

NAMES RELATING TO HIS GREATNESS AND GLORY

Al-'Azim	The Great One
Al-'Aziz	The Mighty One
Al-Qawi	The Most Strong
Al-Qahhār	The Dominant
Al-Jabbār	The Compeller
Al-Mutakabbir	The Majestic
Al-Karim	The Generous One
Al-Hamid	The Praiseworthy
Al-Matin	The Firm One
Az-Zahir	The Manifest
An-Nūr	The Light
Al-Wali	The Protecting Friend
Al-Jalil	The Glorious
Al-Wali	The Governor
Al-Mubin	The Manifest
Al-A'la	The Most High
Al-Qāhir	The Omnipotent
Al-Rafi'	The Sublime
Ghālib	The Predominant
Al-'Aliyy	The Sublime
Al-Majid	The Most Glorious One

NAMES RELATING TO HIS LOVE AND MERCY

Rabb	The Sustainer
Ar-Rahman	The Compassionate
Ar-Rahim	The Merciful
Ar-Ra'uf	The Compassionate
At-Tawwāb	The Accepter of Repentance
Al-Halim	The Clement
Al-'Afuw	The Pardoner
Ash-Shakūr	The Appreciative
As-Salām	The Author of Safety
Al-Mu'min	The Giver of Peace
Al-Barr	The Source of All Goodness
Ar-Razzāq	The Provider
Al-Wahhāb	The Bestower
Al-Wasi'	The All-Embracing
Ash-Shākir	The Appreciative
Al-Akram	The Most Bounteous
An-Nasir	The Helper
Al-Ghaffār	The Great Forgiver
Al-Ghafir	The Forgiver
Al-Hafiyy	The Gracious
Al-Musta'an	One Who is called upon for help: God
Al-Mannān	The Gracious
Al-Kafi	The Sufficient One
Al-Ghafūr	The All-Forgiving
Al-Wādūd	The Loving

NAMES RELATING TO HIS ACT OF CREATION

Al-Khāliq	The Creator
Al-Bari'	The Maker
Al-Musawwir	The Fashioner
Al-Badi'	The Originator
Al-Khallāq	The Creator
Al-Fātir	The Creator

NAMES RELATING TO HIS PERSON

Al-Āhad	The One
Al-Wāhid	The One
Al-Haqq	The Truth
As-Samad	The Eternal
Al-Quddūs	The Holy
Al-Ghani	The Self-Sufficient
Al-Awwal	The First
Al-Akhir	The Last
Al-Hayy	The Alive
Al-Qayyūm	The Self-Subsisting
Allāh	God
Al-ilāh	God

اَعُوْذُ بِوَجْهِ اللهِ الْعَظِيمِ الَّذِى لَيْسَ شَىْءٌ اَعْظَمُ مِنْهُ وَبِكَلِمَاتِ اللهِ التَّامَّاتِ الَّتِى لَا يُجَاوِزُهُنَّ بَرٌّ وَّلَا فَاجِرٌ وَّبِاَسْمَآءِ اللهِ الْحُسْنَى مَا عَلِمْتُ مِنْهَا وَمَا لَمْ اَعْلَمْ مِنْ شَرِّ مَا خَلَقَ وَذَرَاَ وَبَرَاَ۔

I seek refuge in the Countenance of Allāh the Magnificent than Whom naught is more magnificent, in the perfect Words of Allāh which no saint nor sinner can outstrip, and in the fair names of Allāh which I know or know not, from the evil of that which He hath created and scattered, or formed out of naught.

باسْمِكَ اللّٰهُمَّ اَمُوتُ وَاَحْيَا

In Thy name, O my Allah: I shall die and in Thy name I shall live.

رَبَّنَا اٰتِنَا فِى الدُّنْيَا حَسَنَةً وَّفِى الْاٰخِرَةِ حَسَنَةً وَّقِنَا عَذَابَ النَّارِه

Our Lord ! Give unto us (that which is) good in this world, and (that which is) good in the Hereafter, and save us from the torment of Hell-Fire.

وَلِلّٰهِ الْحَمْدُ اَوَّلًا وَّاٰخِرًا وَّظَاهِرًا وَّبَاطِنًا

Praise be to Allah Who is the First and the Last, the Obvious and the Immanent.

رَبَّنَا لَا تُؤَاخِذْنَا اِنْ نَّسِيْنَا اَوْ اَخْطَأْنَا

Our Lord ! take us not to task, if we forget, or we make mistake.

رَبَّنَا تَقَبَّلْ مِنَّا اِنَّكَ اَنْتَ السَّمِيْعُ الْعَلِيْمُ

Our Lord ! Accept this (service) from us. Behold, it is Thou Who are the Hearer, the Knower.

اَللّٰهُمَّ صَلِّ عَلٰى مُحَمَّدٍ سَيِّدِ الْمُرْسَلِيْنَ وَاٰلِهِ وَاَصْحَابِهٖ اَجْمَعِيْنَ

O Allah ! shower Thy blessings upon Muhammad, the Chief of the Messengers and upon his posterity and his companions.